AF353162

The flowers are a mystery of nature that is revealed to man. They have always been symbols of harmony, life and beauty. They appear in these Mae Jeon works as digital prints, now modified according to the narrative requirement of the artist who uses the expressive power of the computer as she likes. The light tends to the surreal and gives full thickness to the protagonists by making them alive and dynamic and not static figurations. Full of pathos, the flowers of the artist Mae Jeon brings a universal message of harmony and balance which is really very pleasant and valued.

I fiori un mistero della natura che si svela all'uomo. Essi da sempre sono simboli di armonia, vita e bellezza. Appaiono in questi lavori di Mae Jeon sotto forma di stampa digitale, ora modificati secondo l'esigenza narrativa dell'artista che usa la forza espressiva del calcolatore a suo piacimento. La luce tende al surreale e dona corposo spessore ai protagonisti rendendoli vivi e dinamici e non statiche figurazioni. Pieni di pathos, i fiori dell'artista Mae Jeon sono portatori di un messaggio universale di armonia ed equilibrio davvero molto piacevole e ricercato.

Dino Marasà

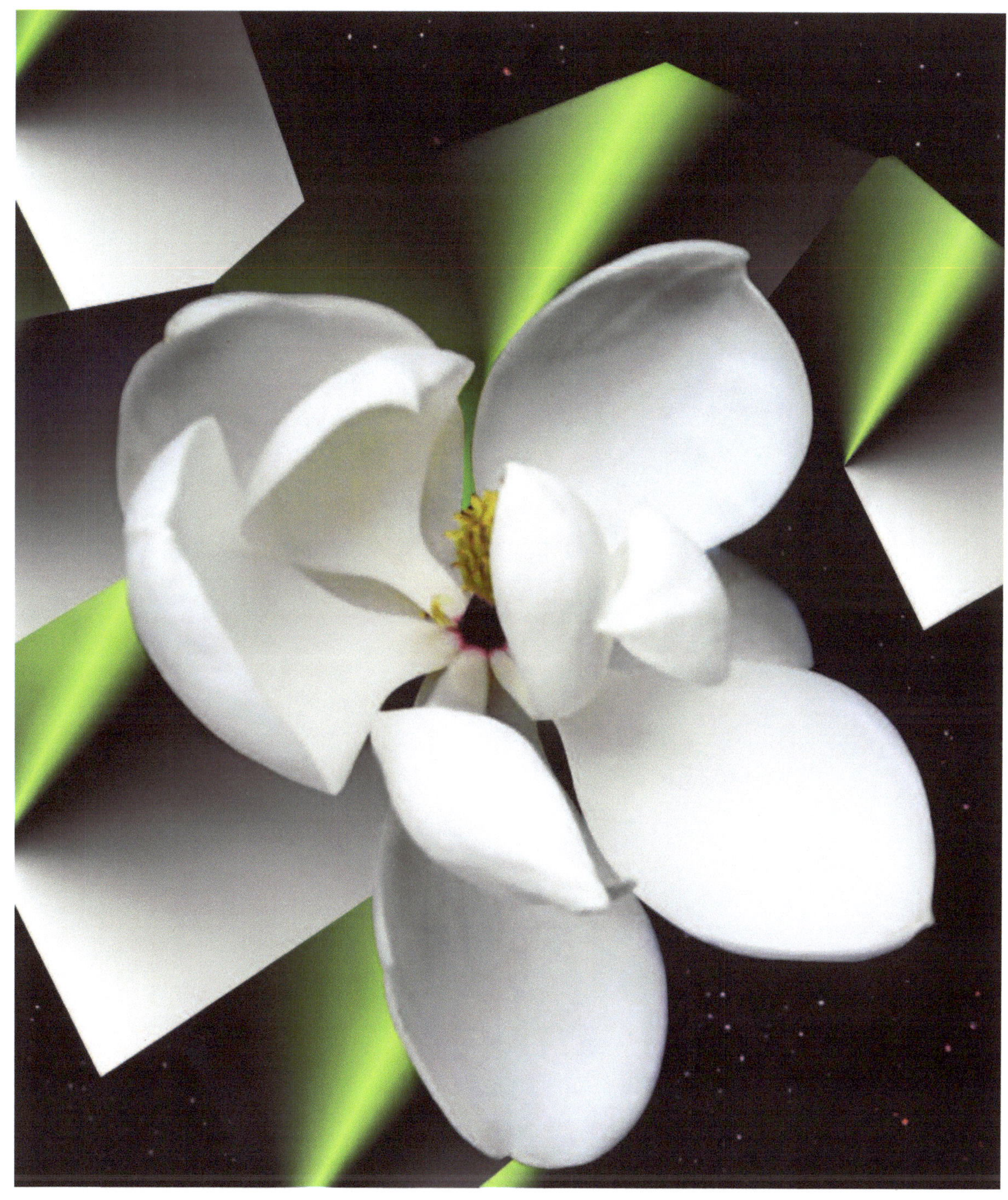

Absolute Virtue, digital print on canvas, 24x20 inch

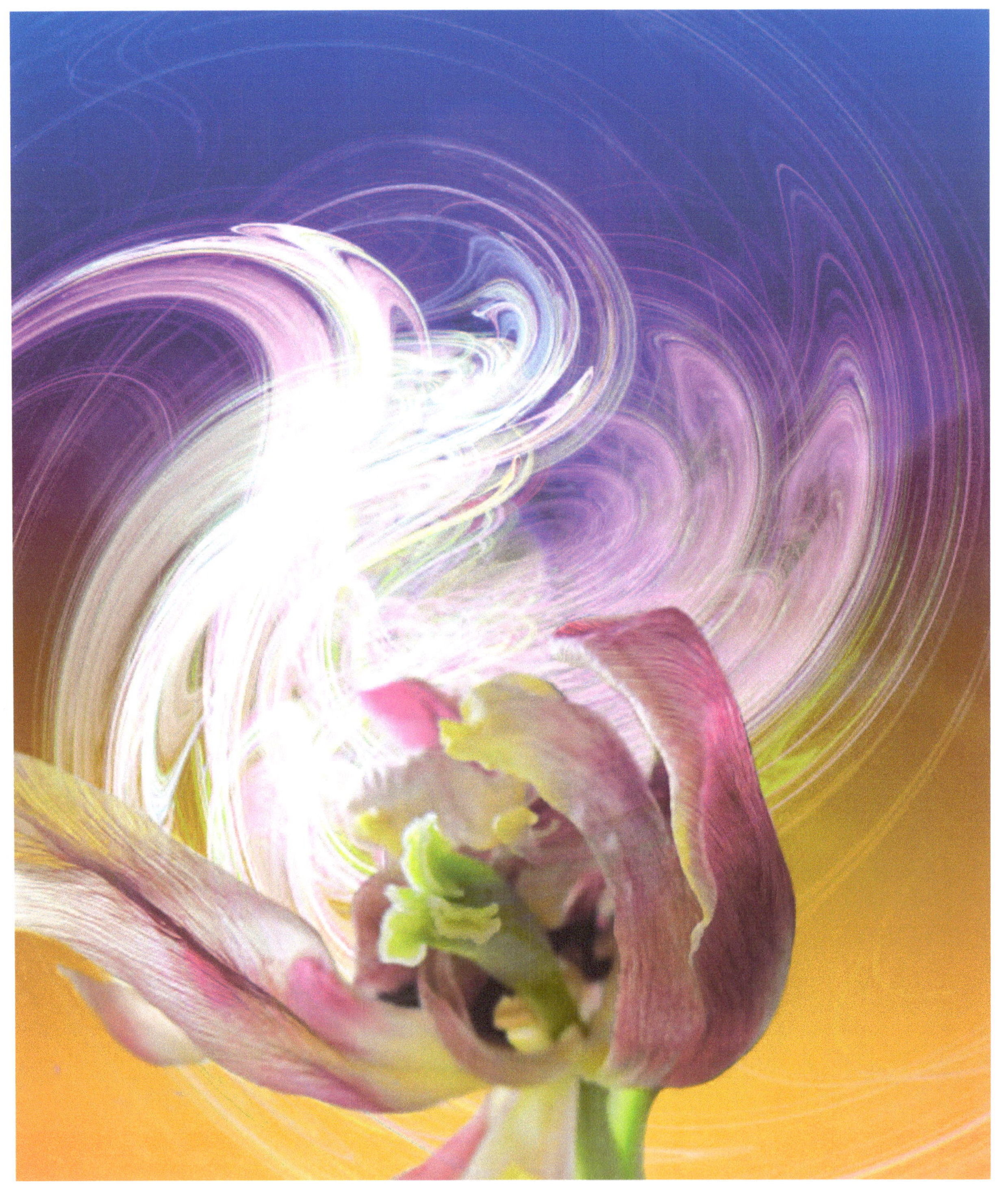

Willing Mind,
digital print on canvas
24x20 inch

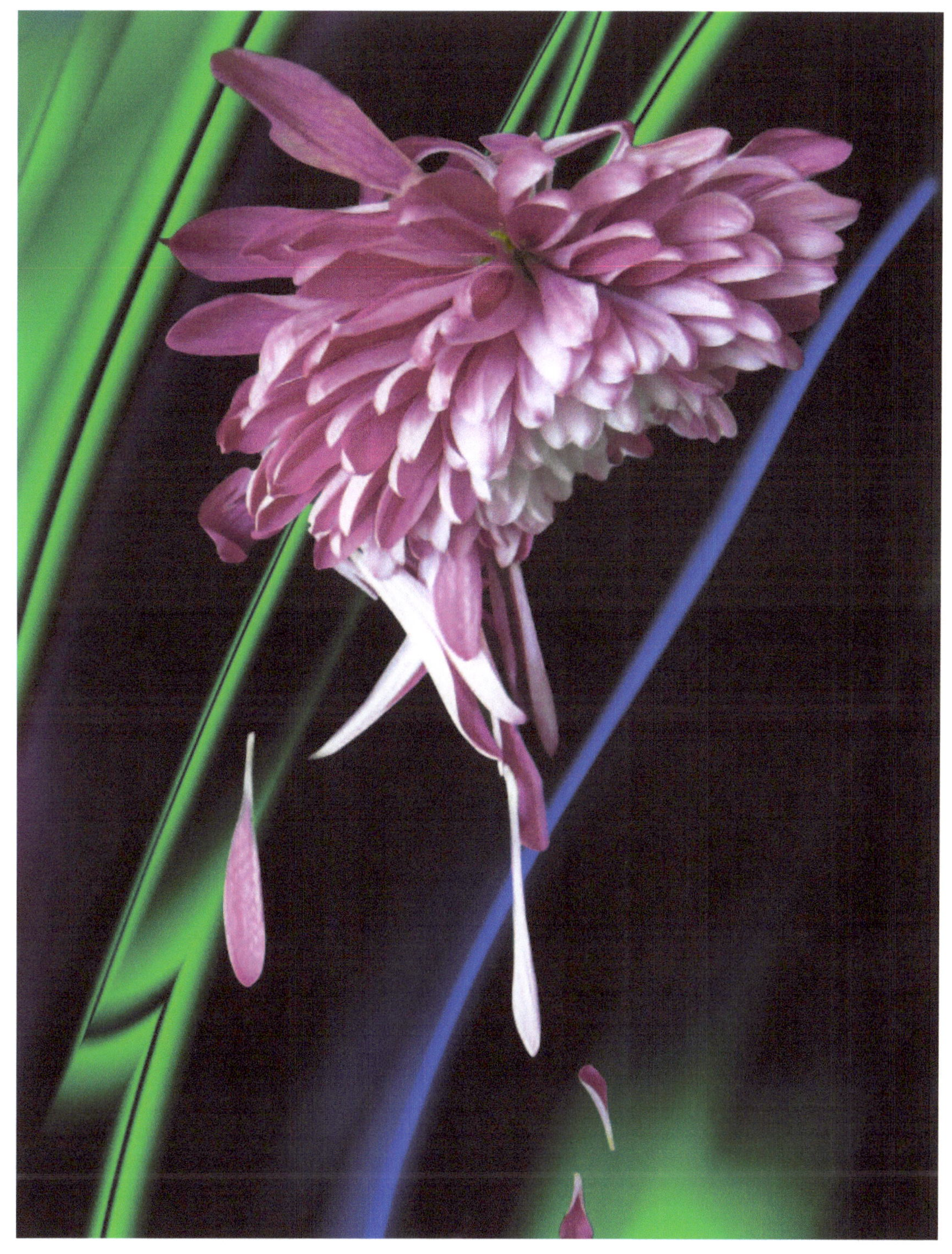

Falling Time
digital print on canvas
24x18 inch

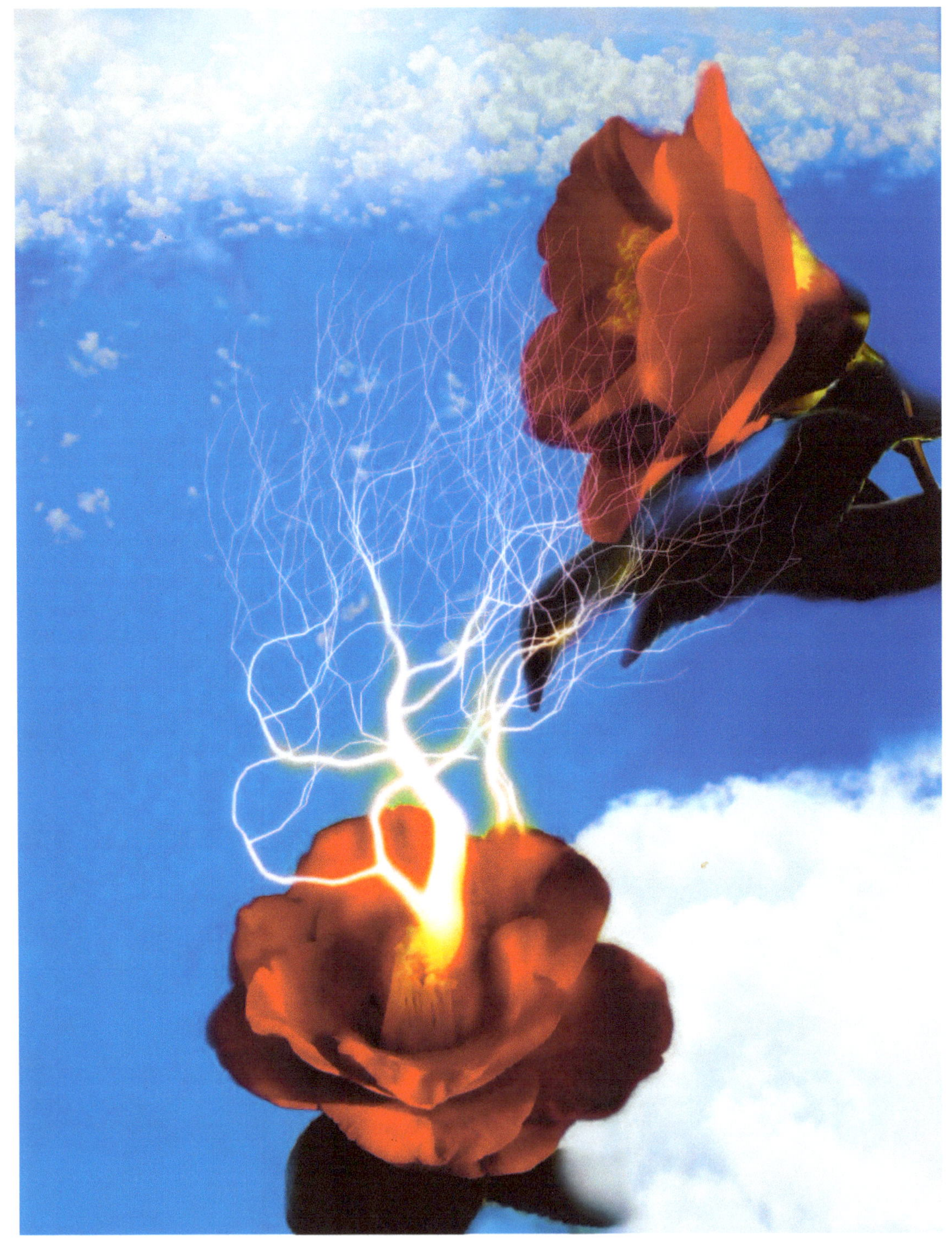

Telepathy
digital print on canvas
24x18 inch

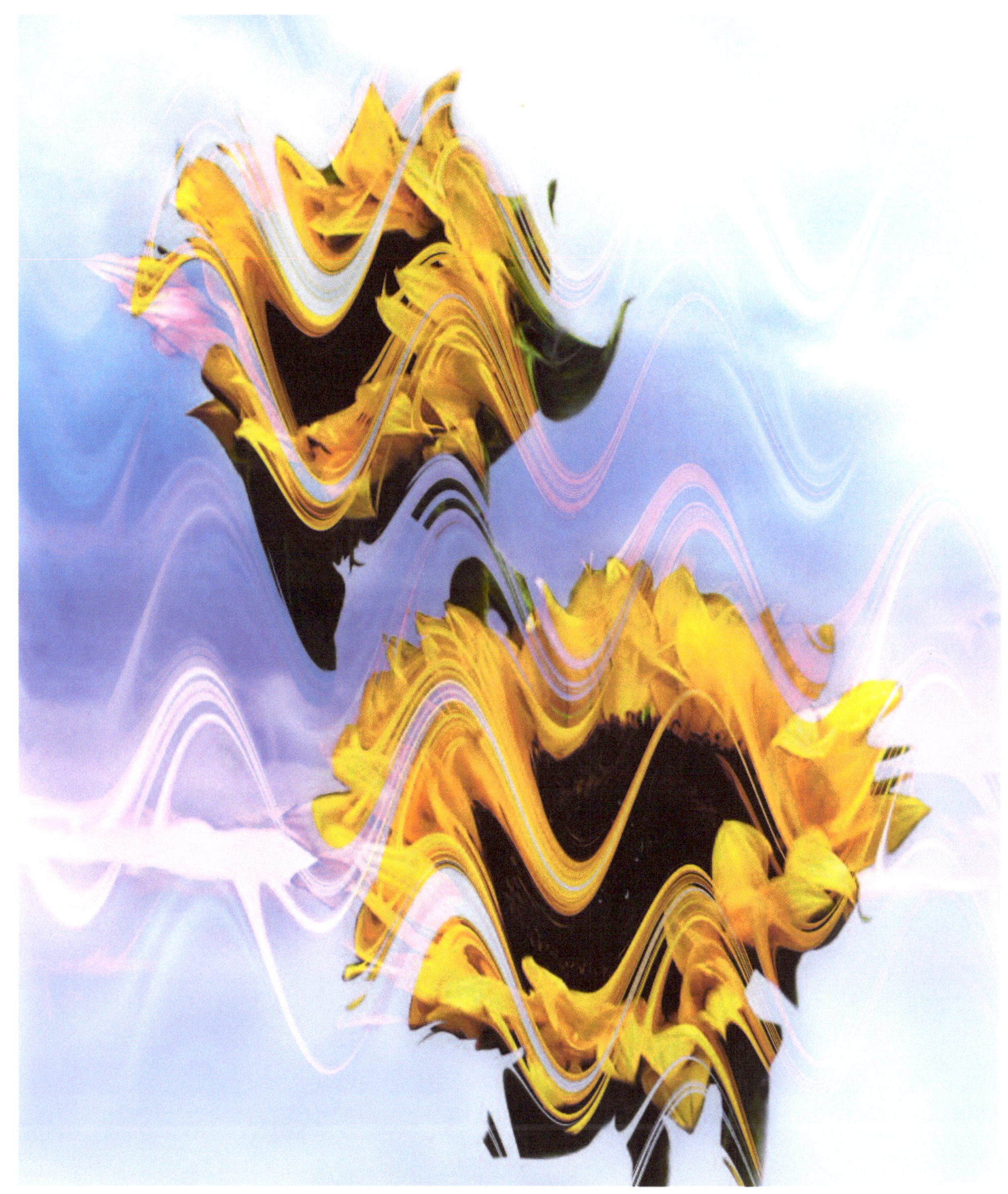

Spiritual Wave
digital print on canvas
24x20 inch

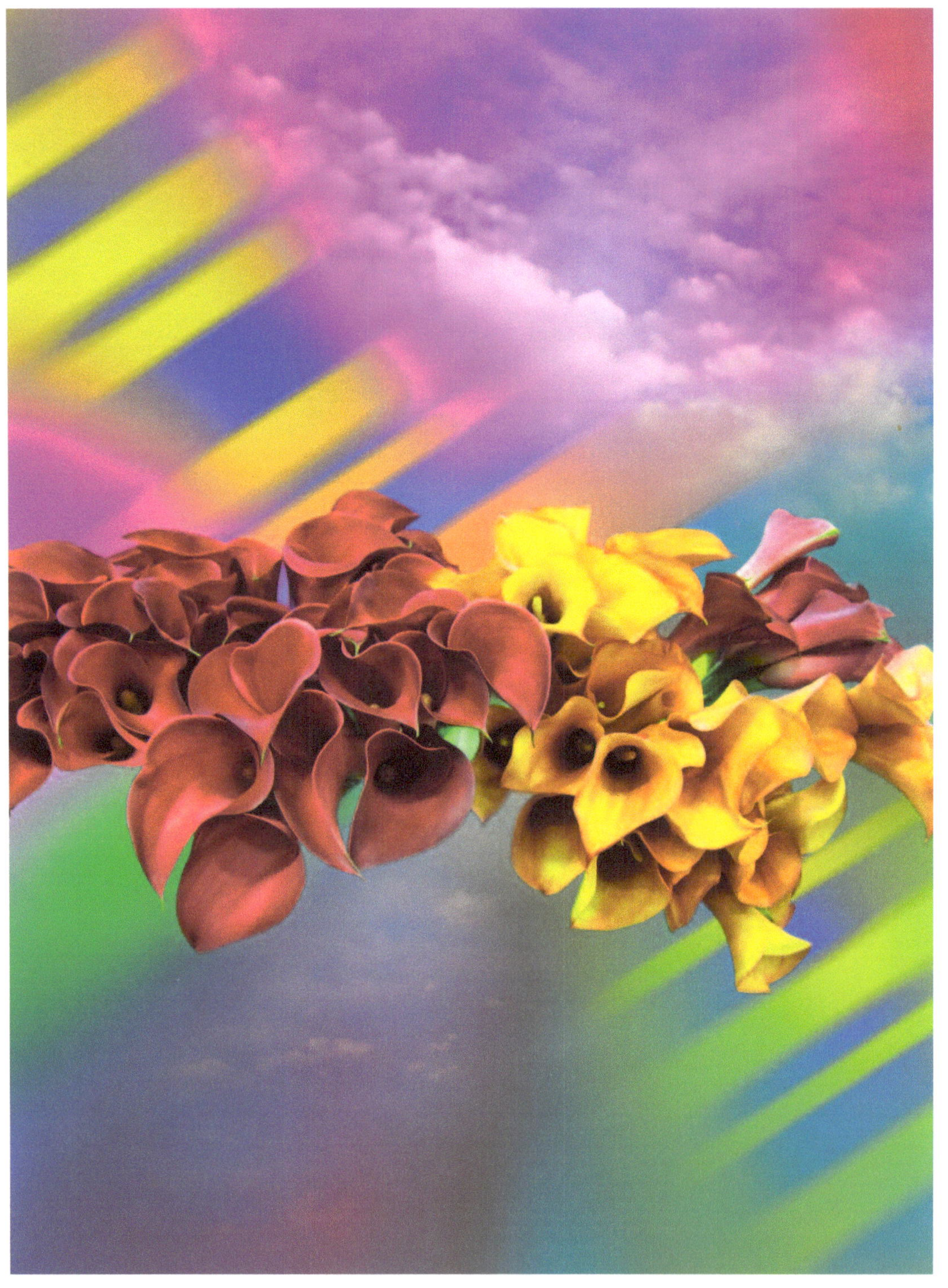

Heavenly Triumph
digital print on canvas
36x24 inch

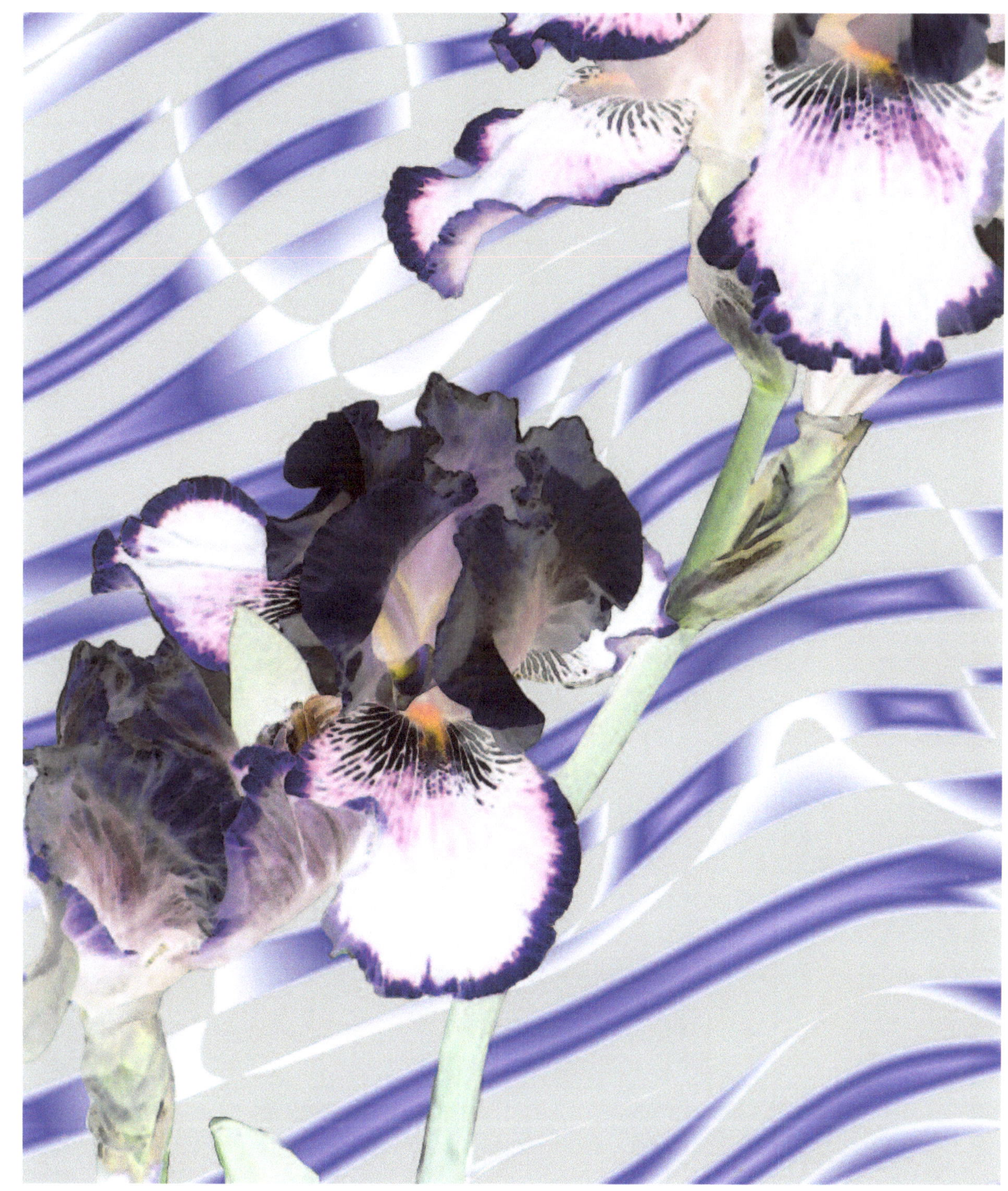

Healing Wave
digital print on metal
24x20 inch

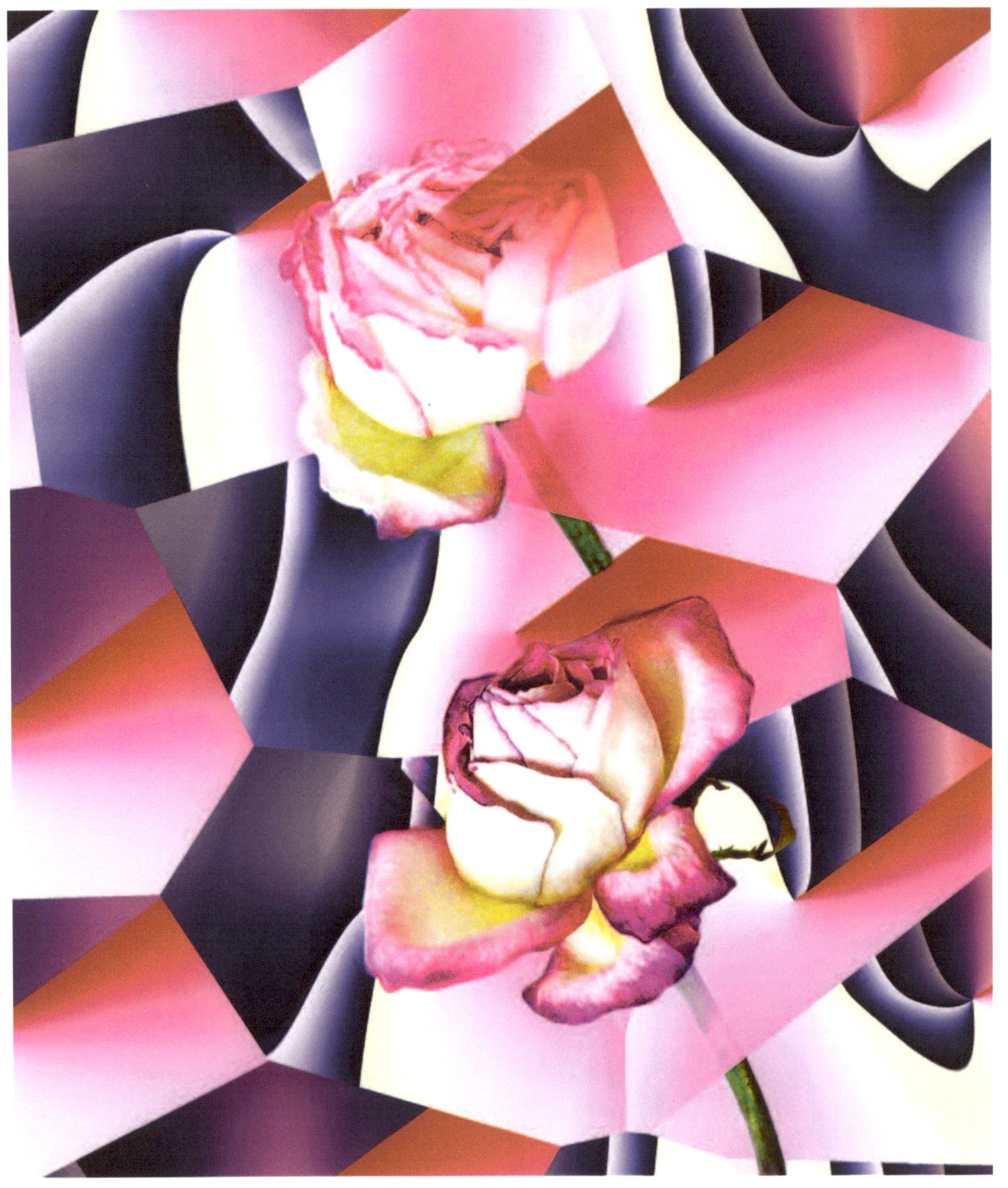

Preserved Beauty
digital print on canvas
24x20 inch

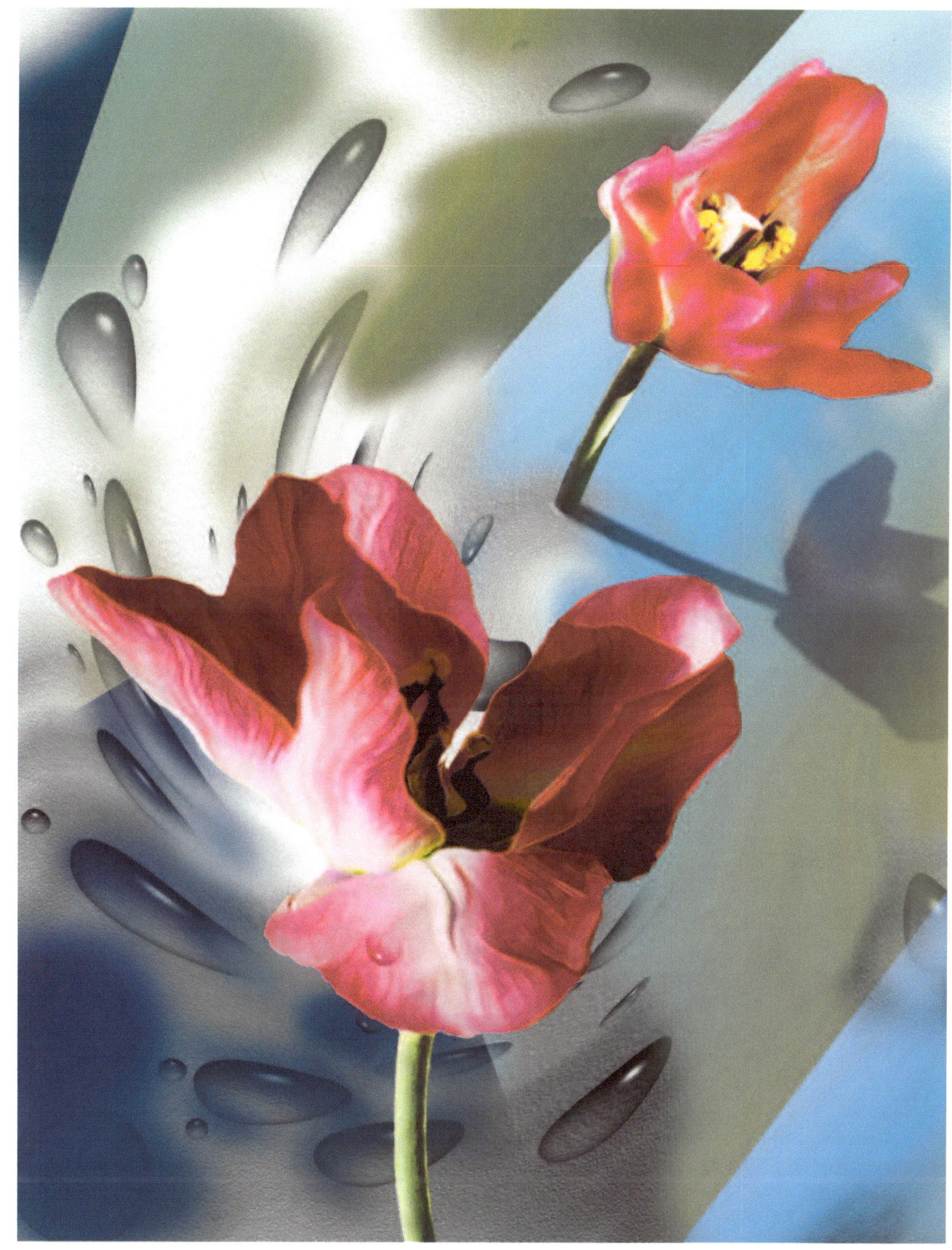

Thirst in Splash
digital print on canvas
24x18 inch

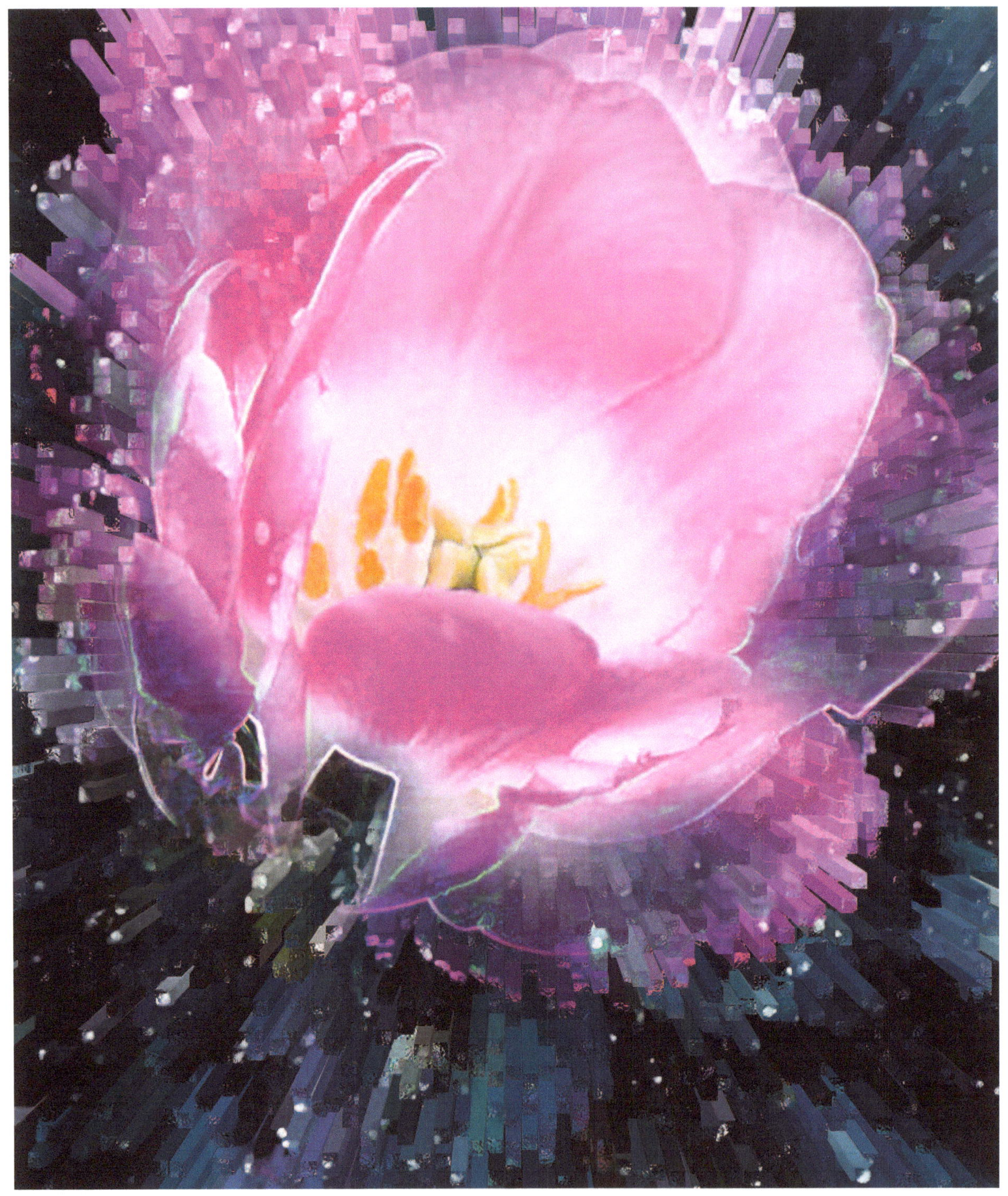

Bursting Hope
digital print on canvas
24x20 inch

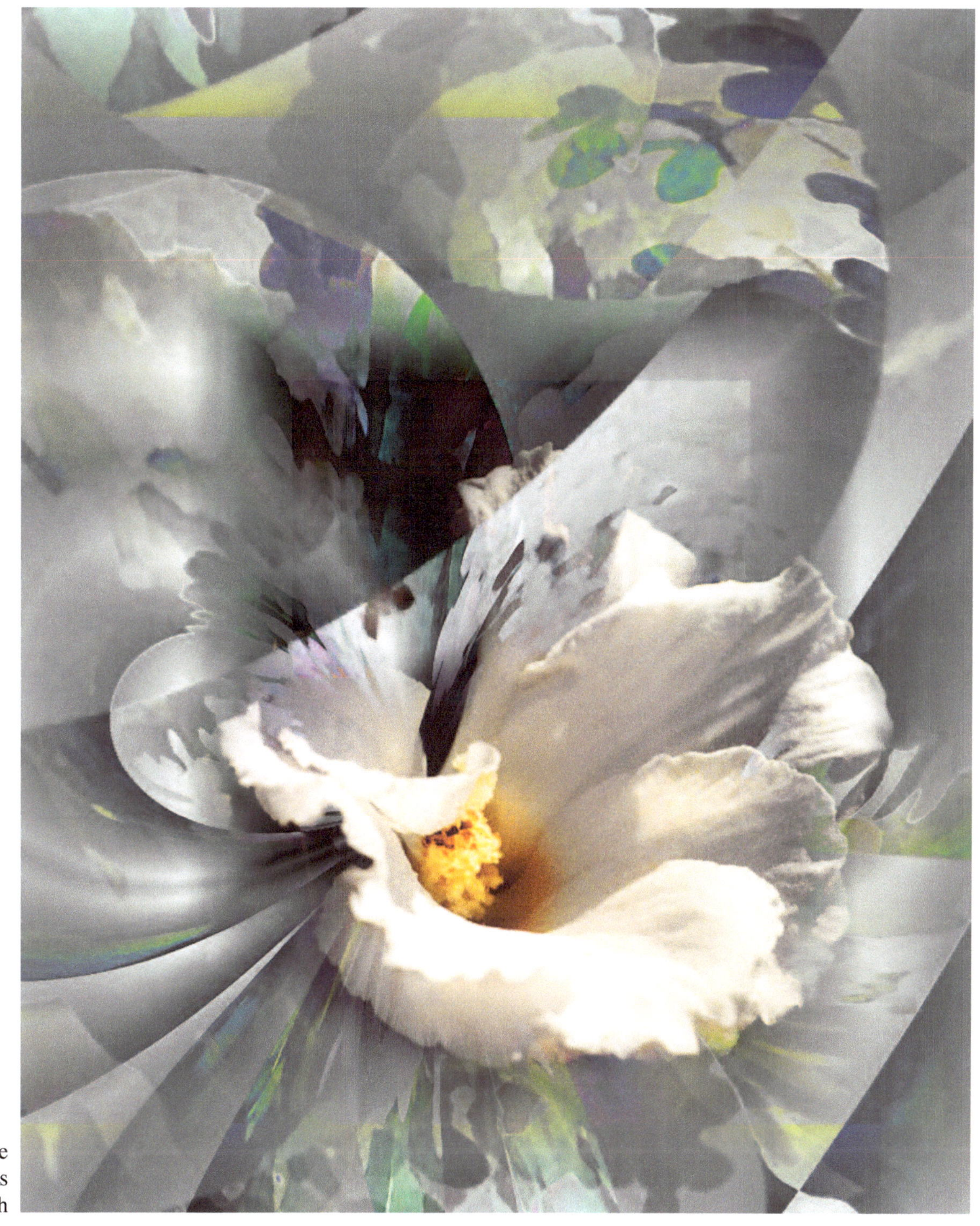

Source of Hope
digital print on canvas
24x20 inch

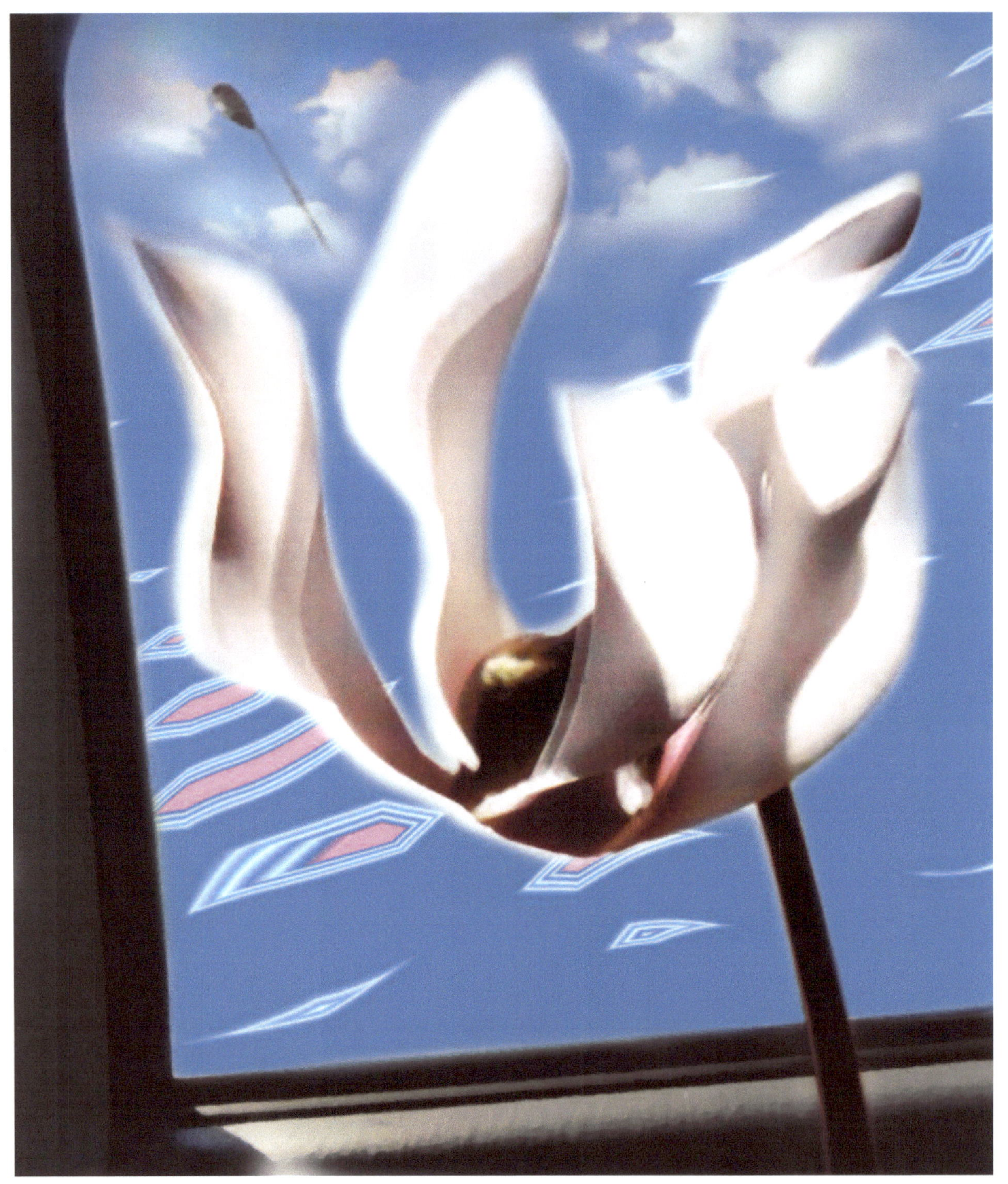

Returning
digital print on canvas
24x20 inch

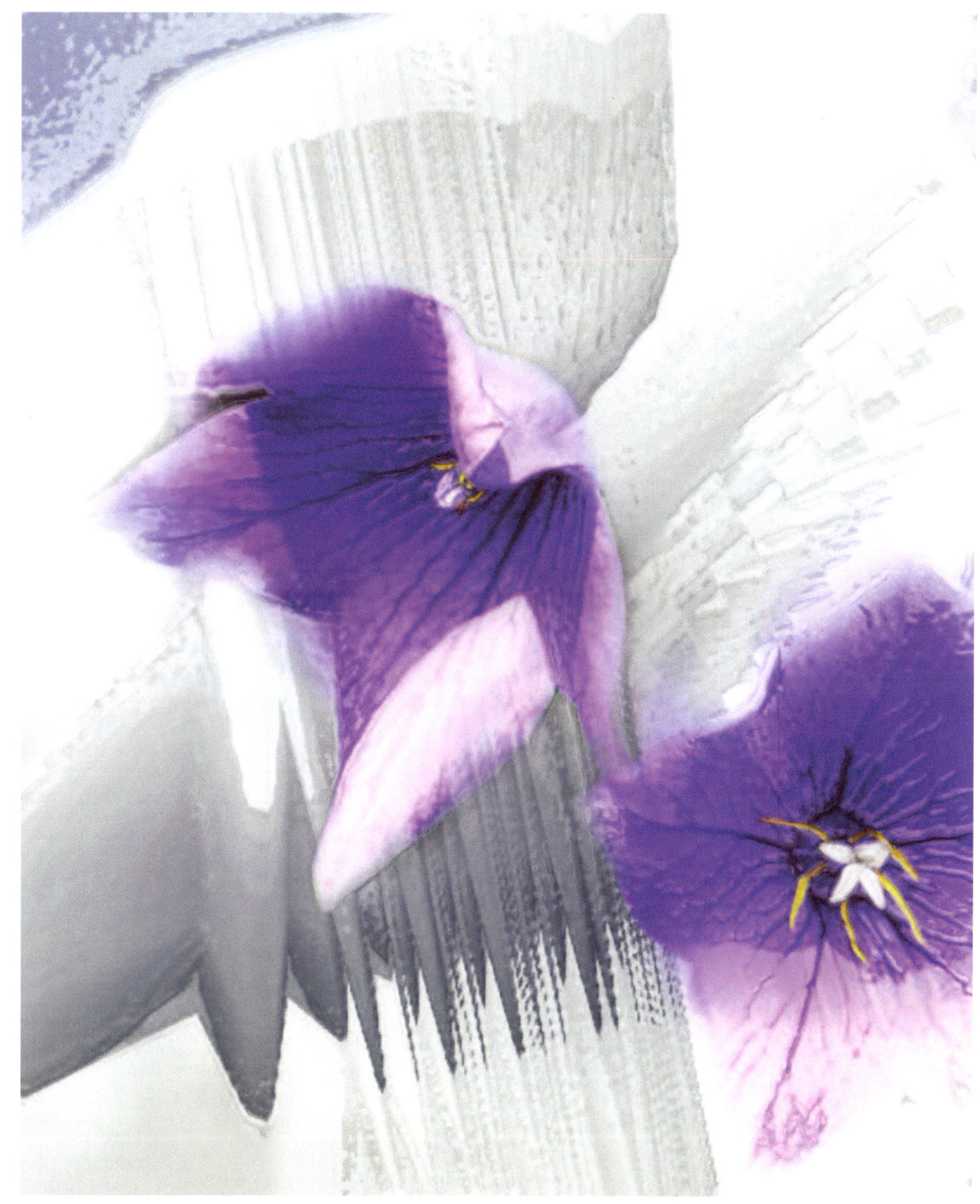

Frozen Passion
digital print on canvas
24x20 inch

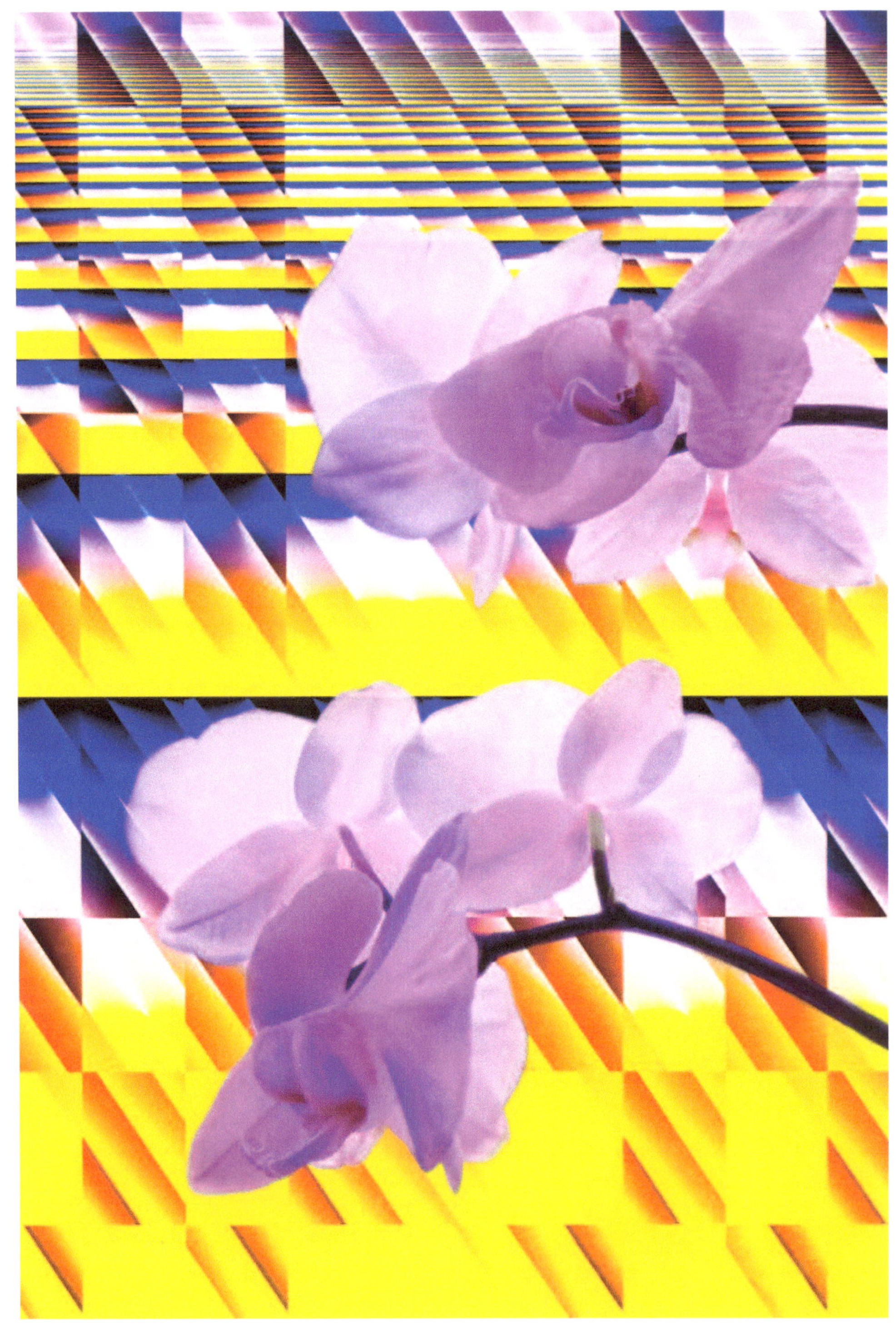

Foreseen
digital print on canvas
30x20 inch

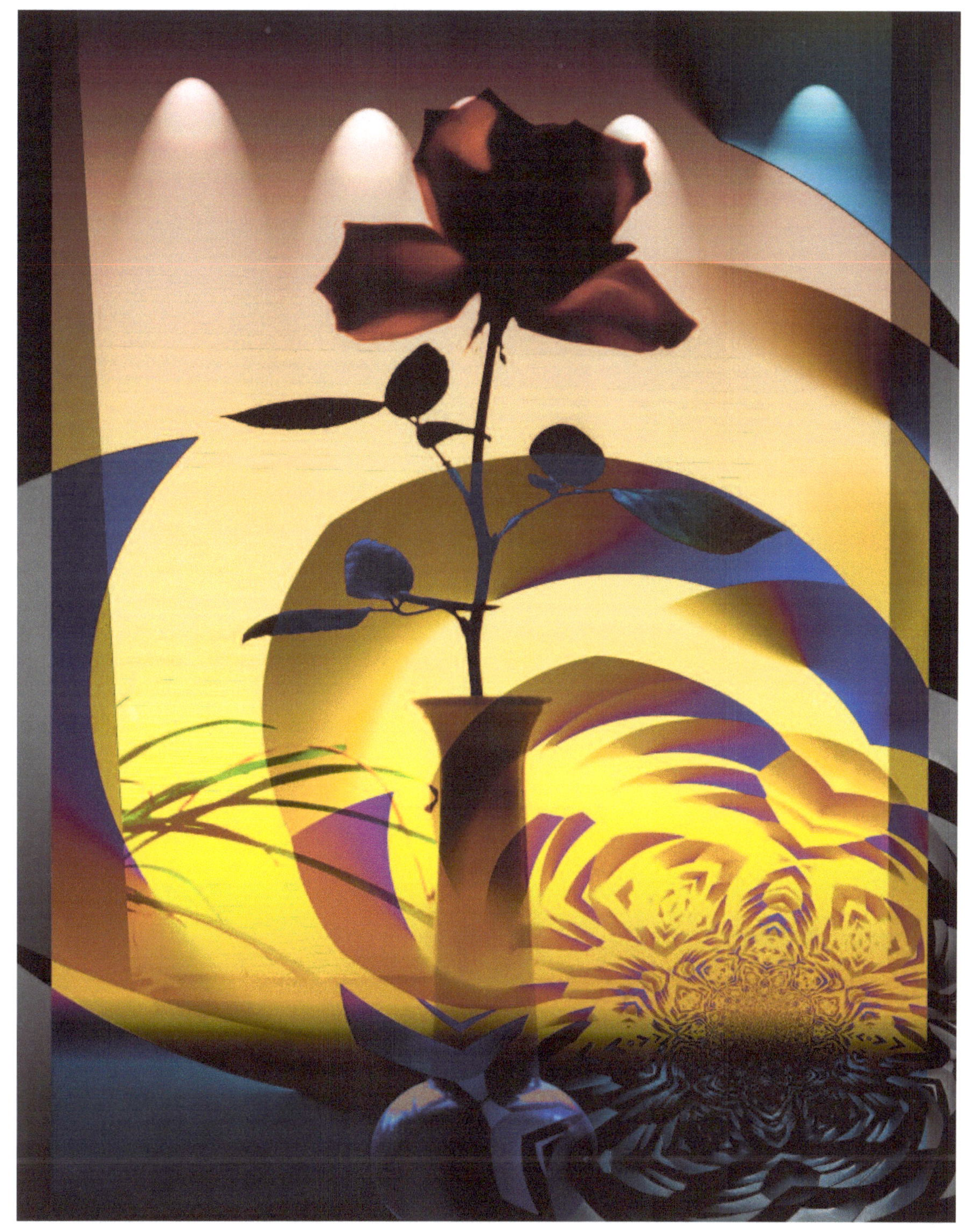

Night Lights
digital print on canvas
26x20 inch

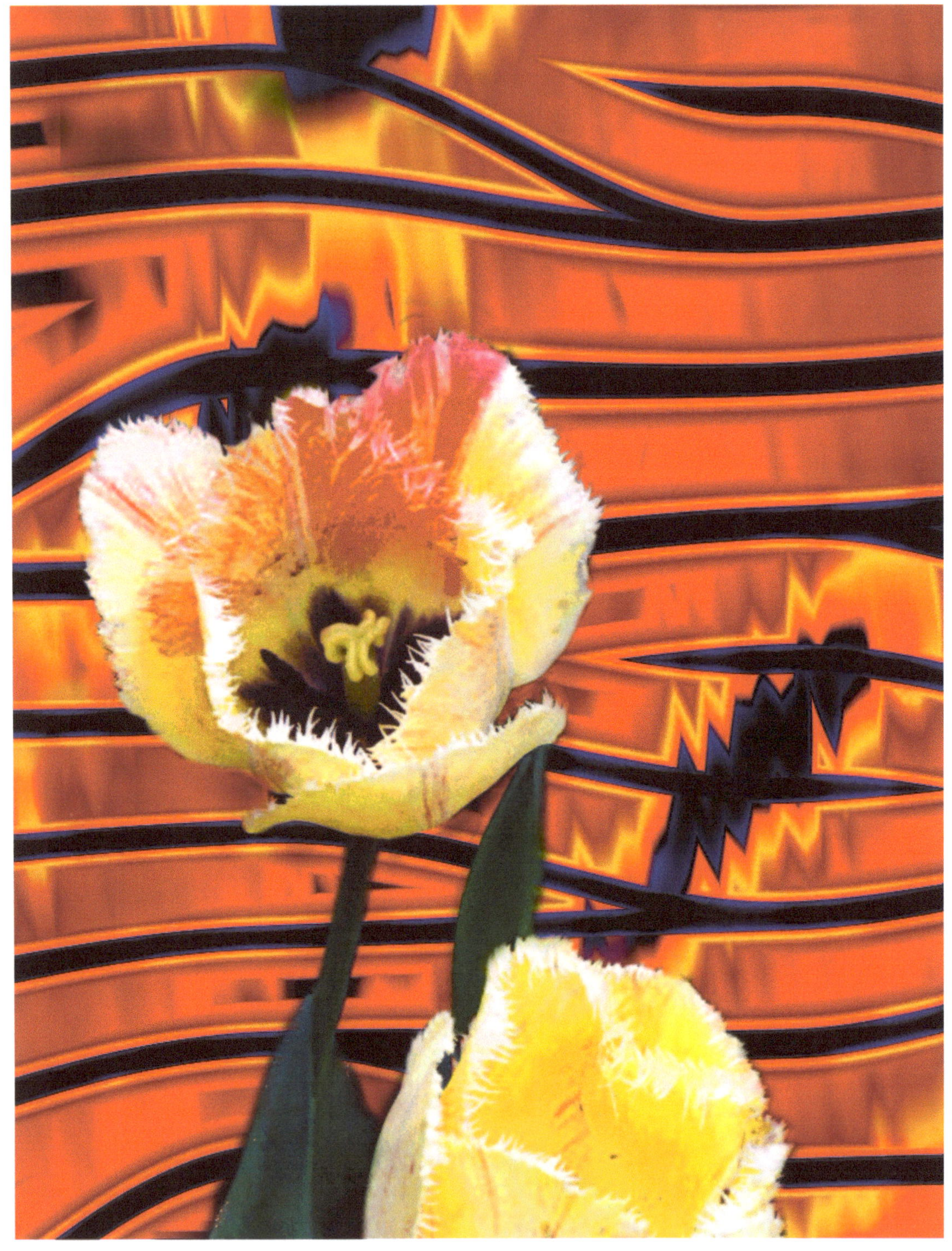

Unceasing Zeal
digital print on canvas
24x18 inch

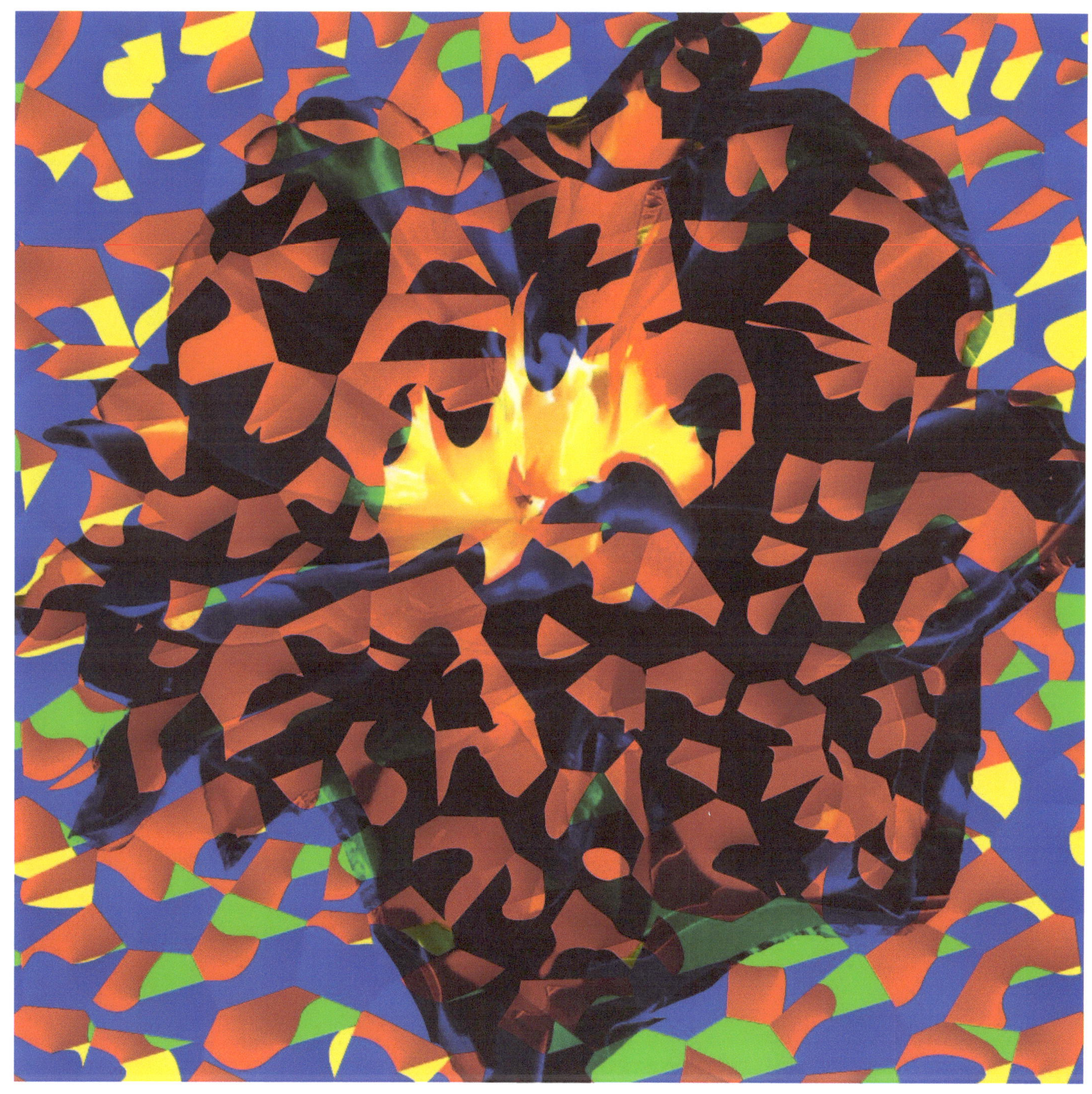

Core Desire, digital print on metal, 24x24 inch

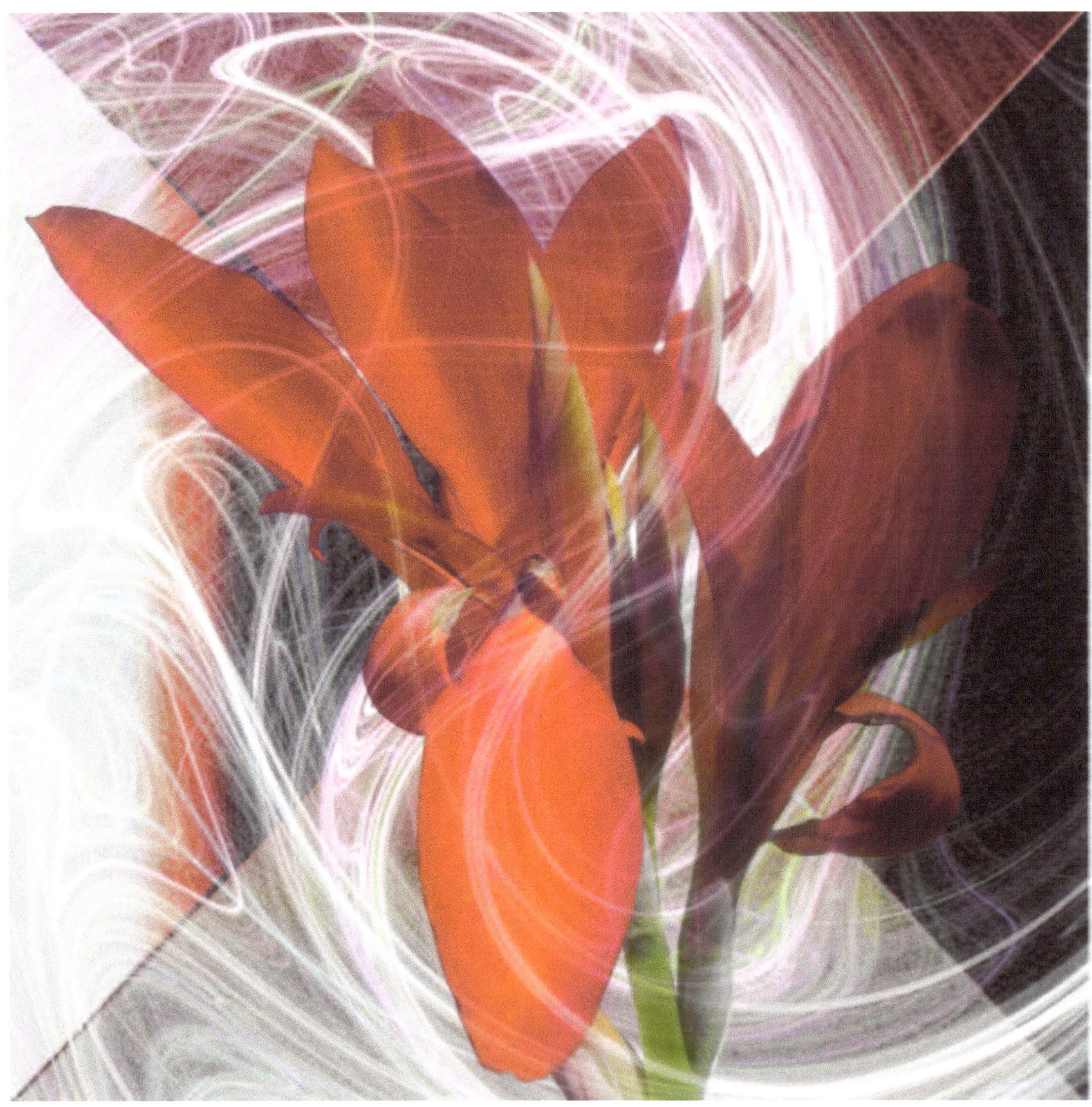

Divine Tongue, digital print on canvas, 18x18 inch

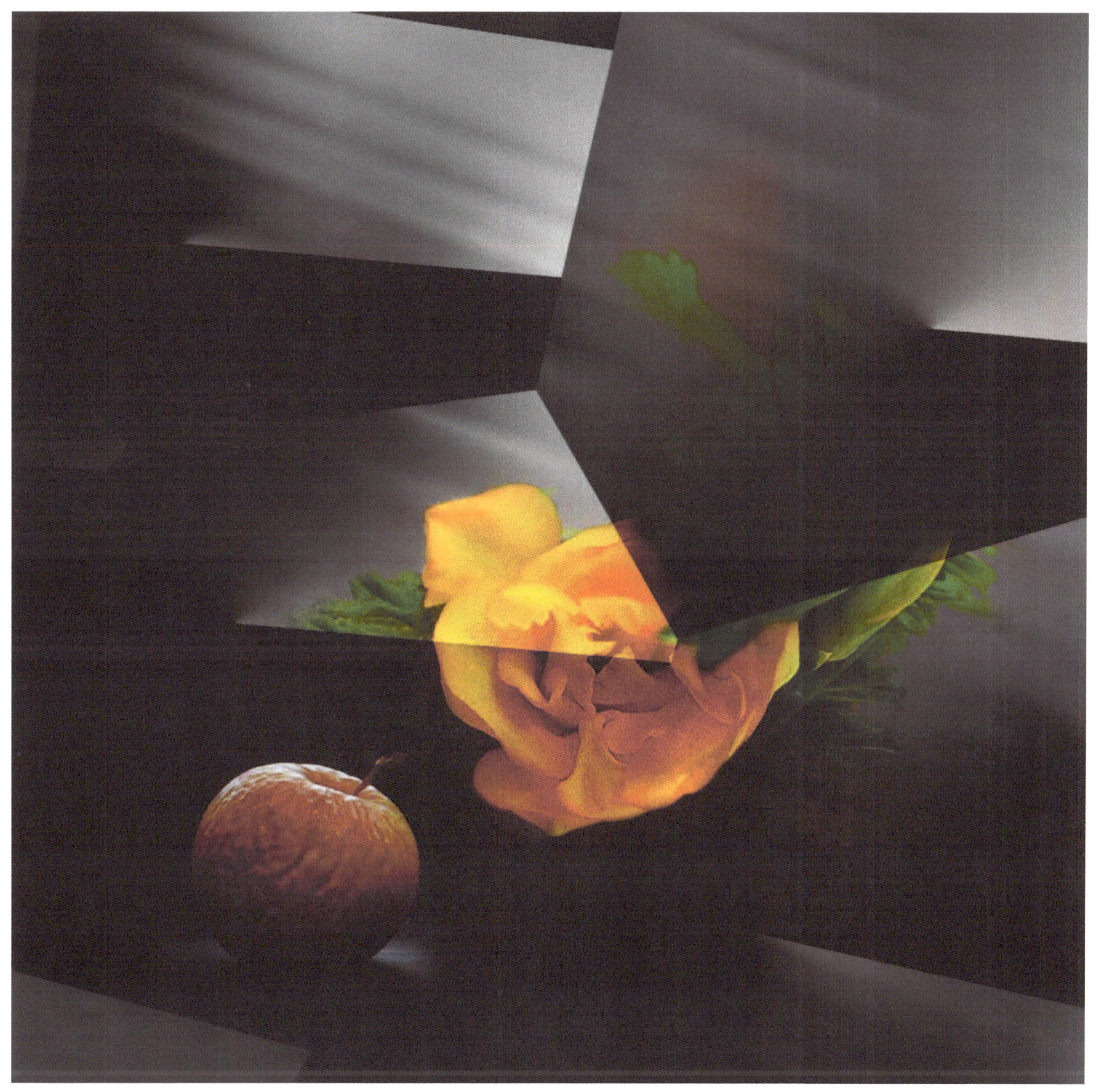

Interlude, digital print on canvas, 24x24 inch

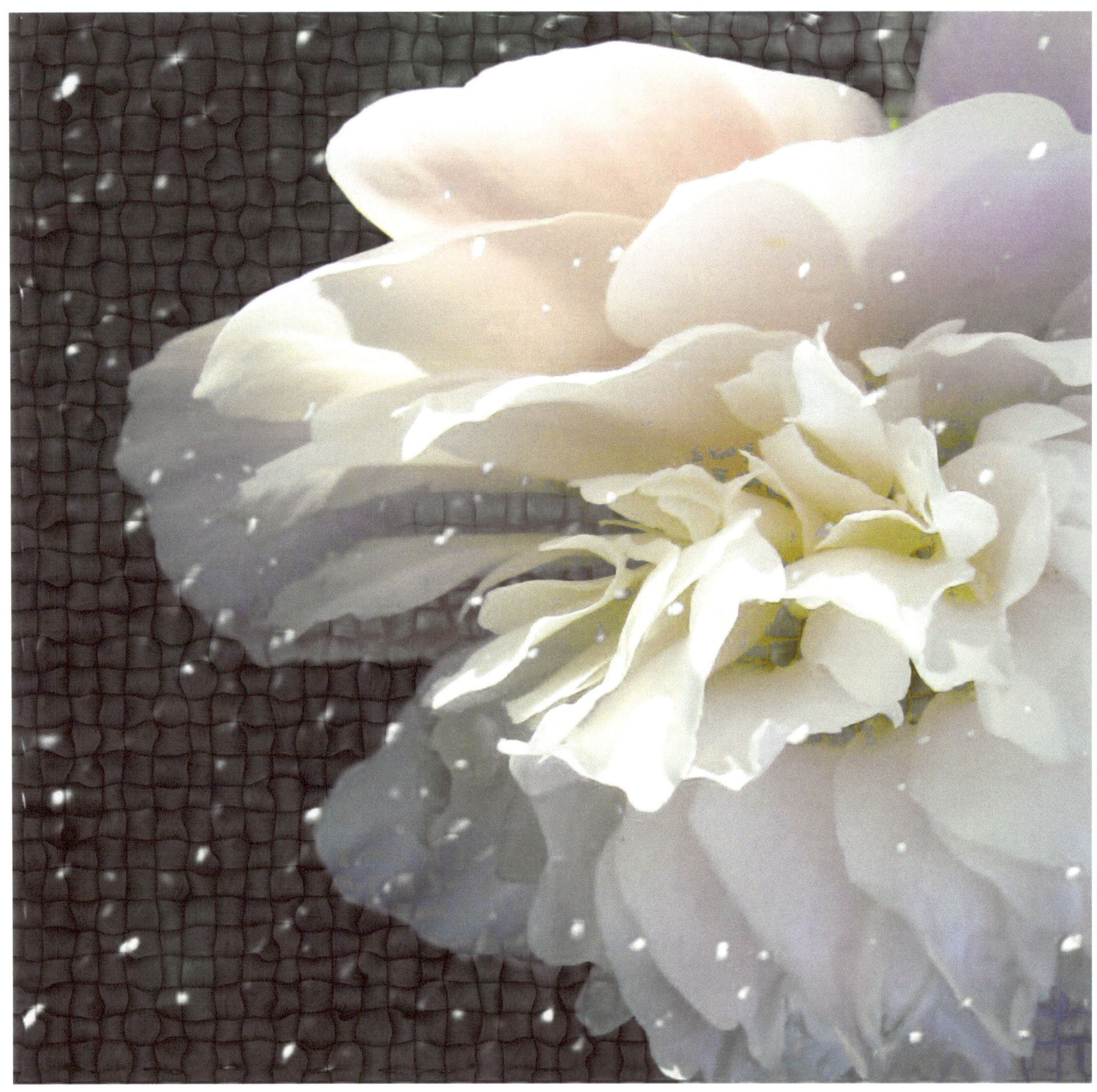

Inspirit, digital print on metal, 24x24 inch

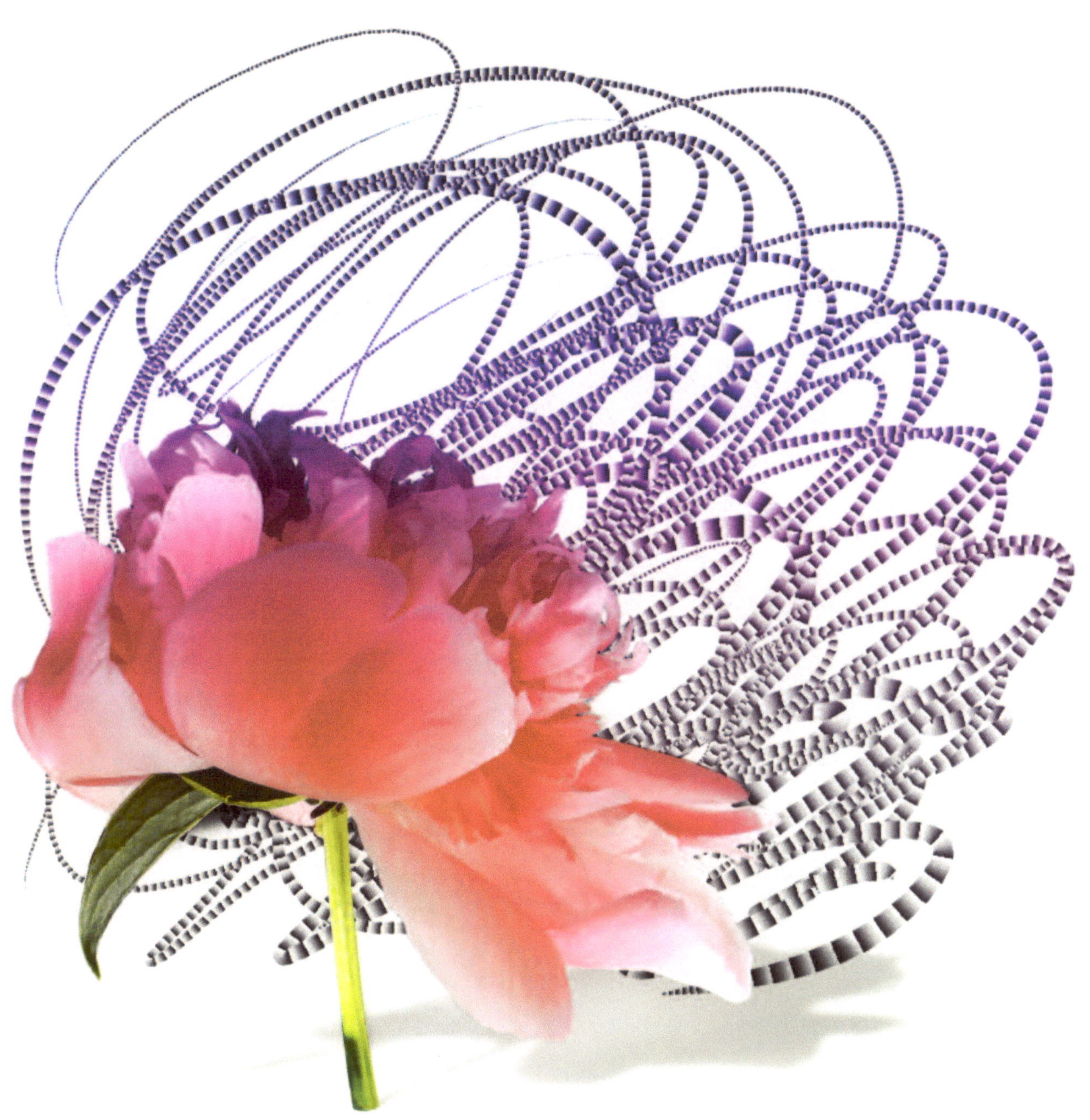

Extra Perception, digital print on canvas, 30x30 inch

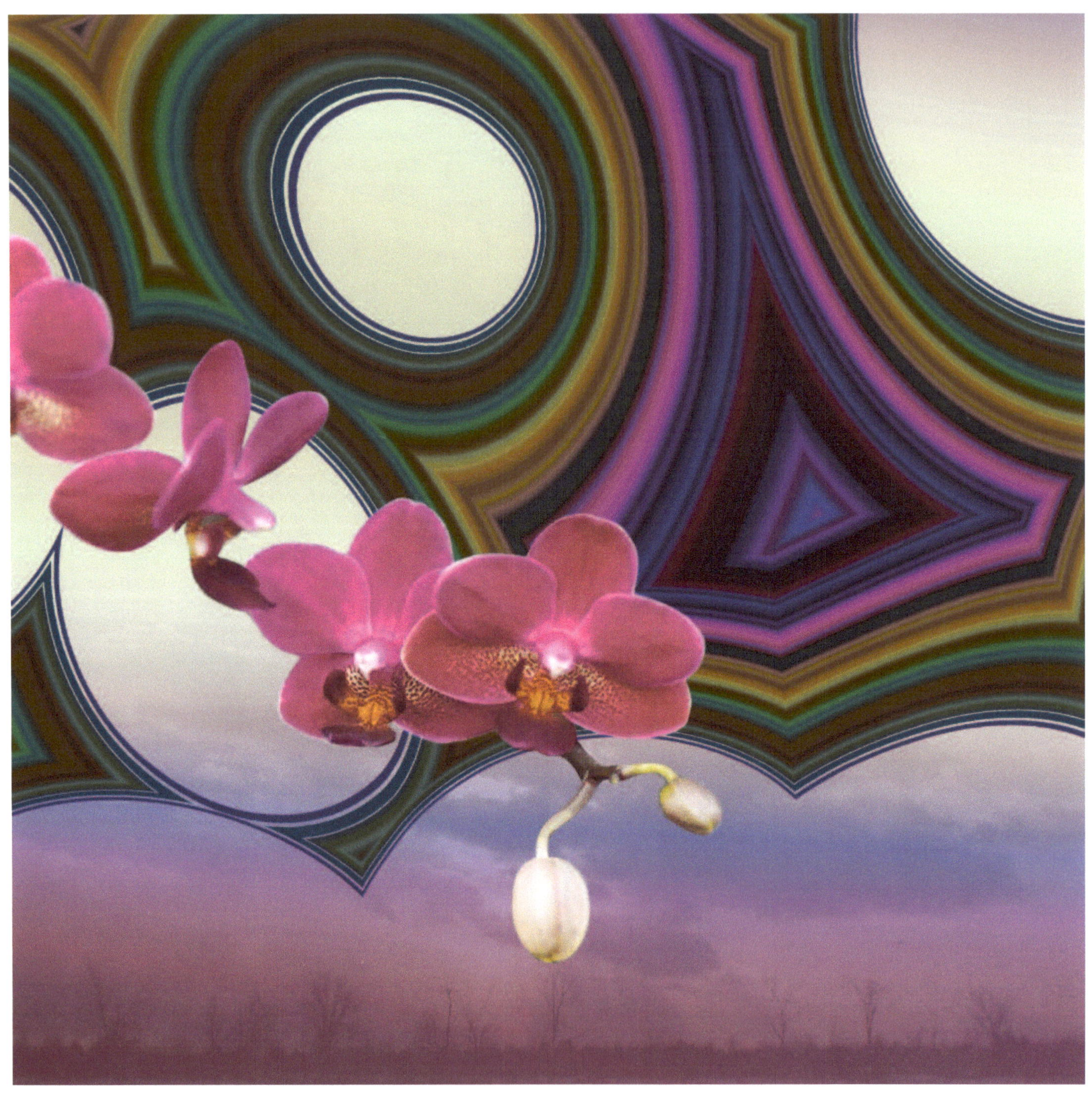

Descending Grace, digital print on canvas, 24x24 inch

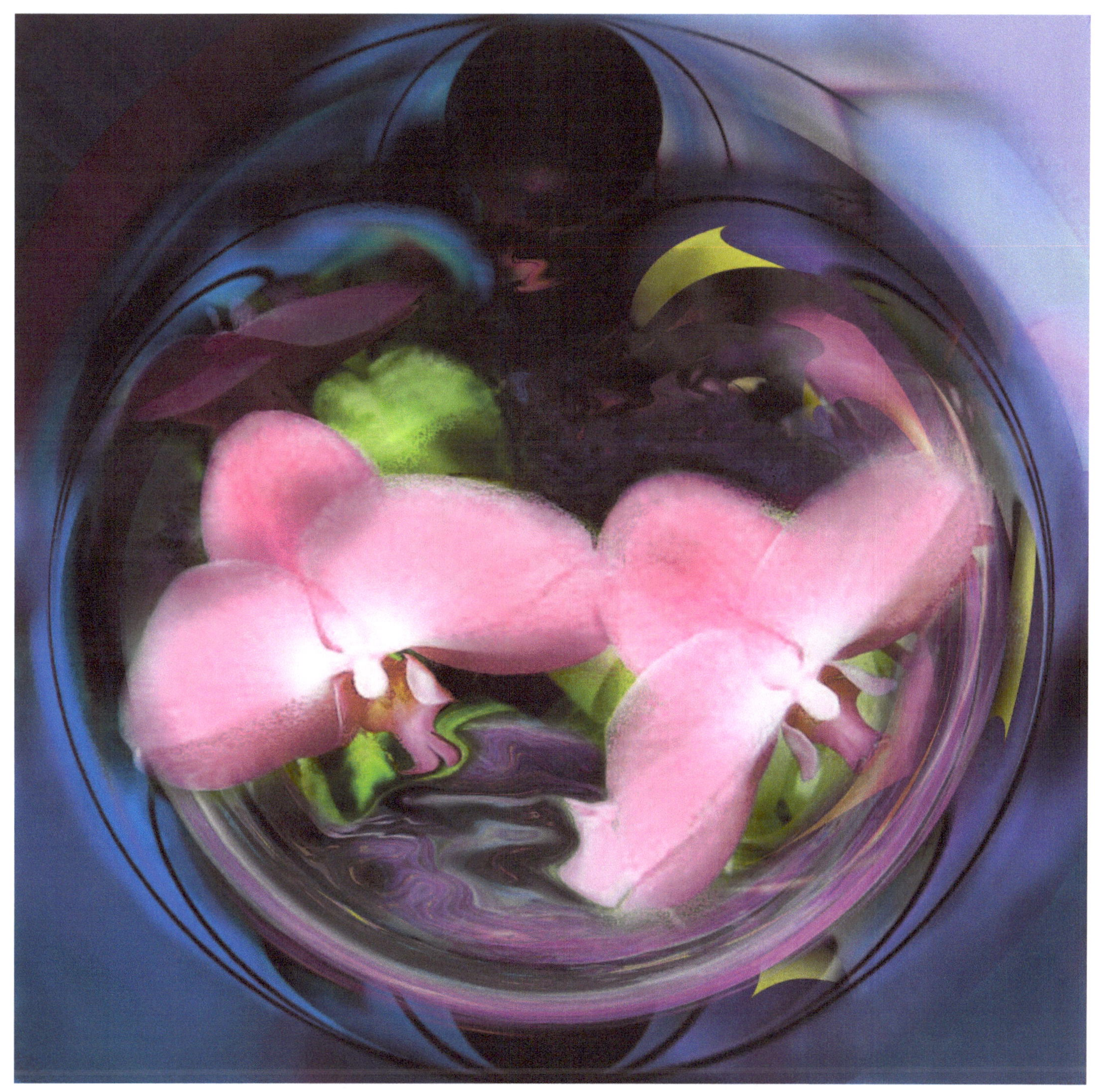

Longing Spirit, digital print on canvas, 24x24 inch

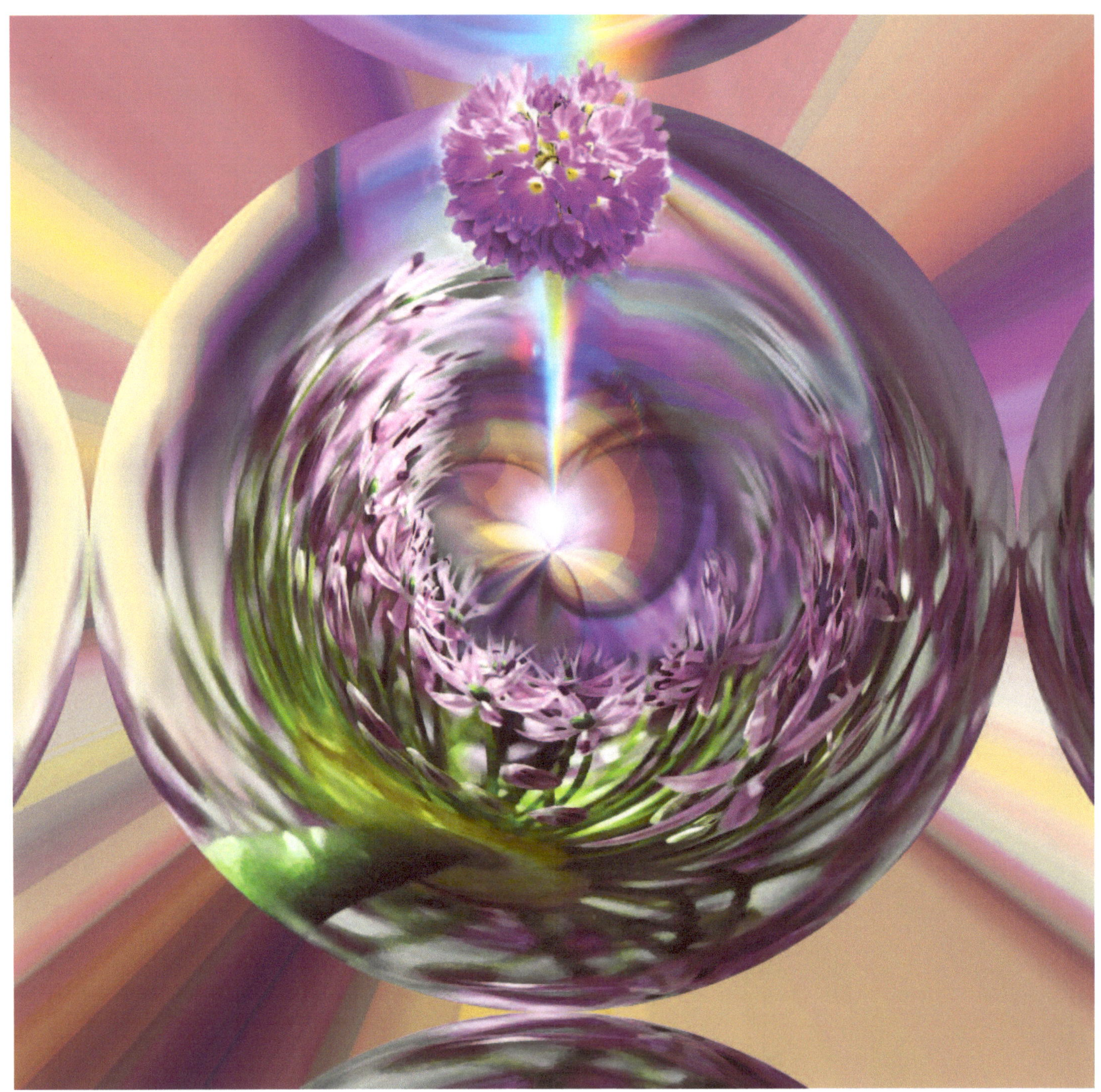

Ultimate Object, digital print on canvas, 24x24 inch

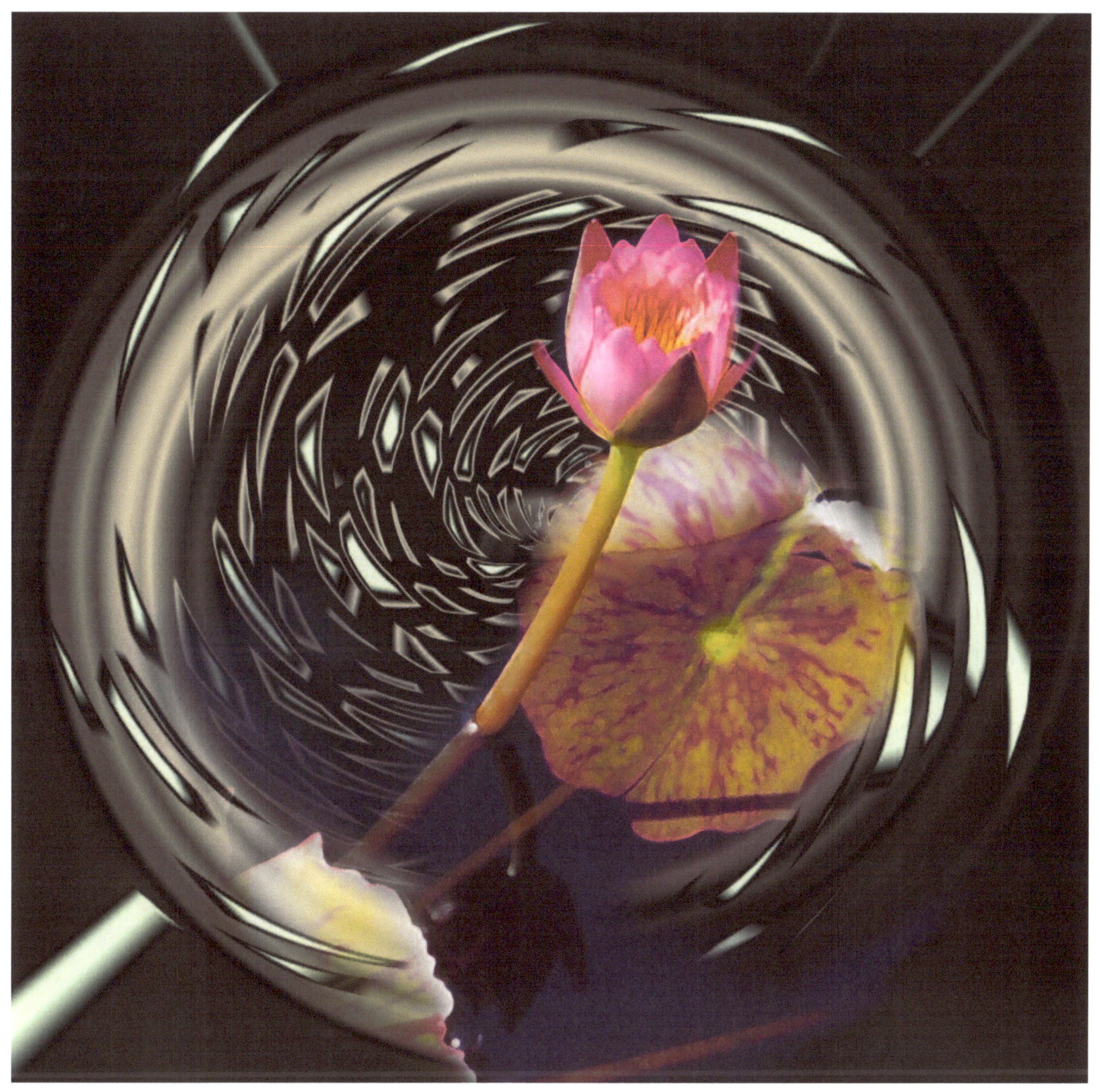

Wishing Well, digital print on canvas, 24x24 inch

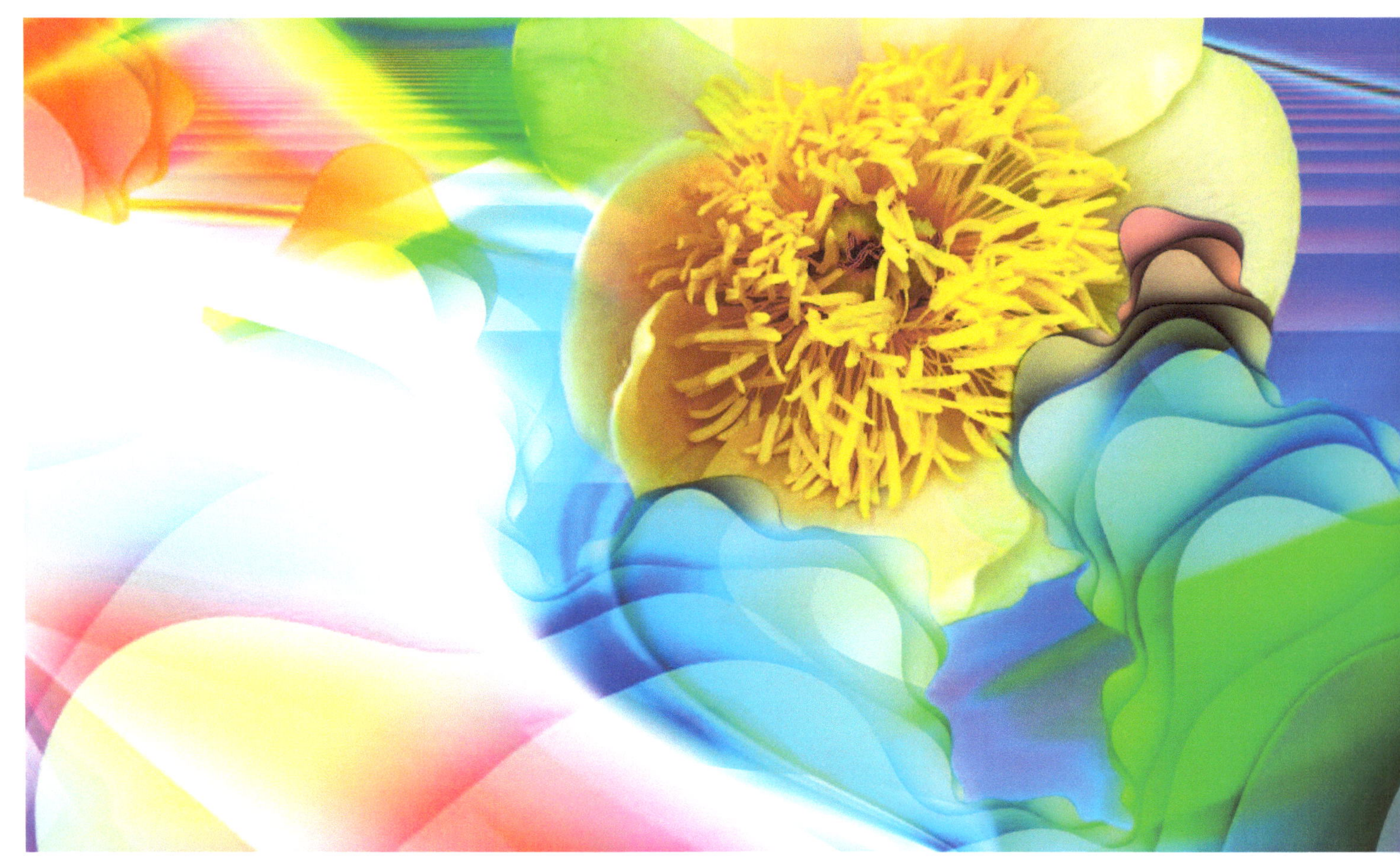

Streaming Hope, digital print on canvas, 25x42 inch

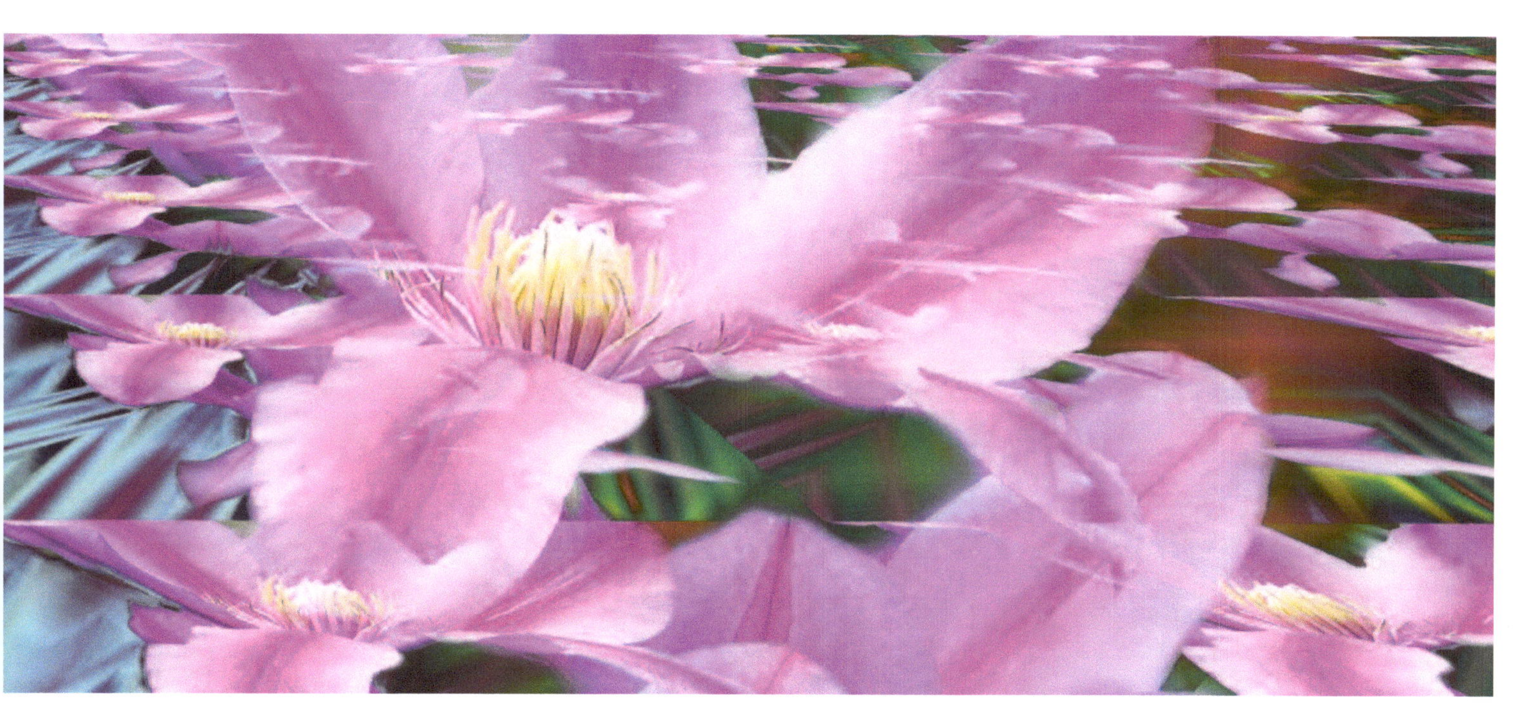

High Spirits, digital print on metal, 16x36 inch

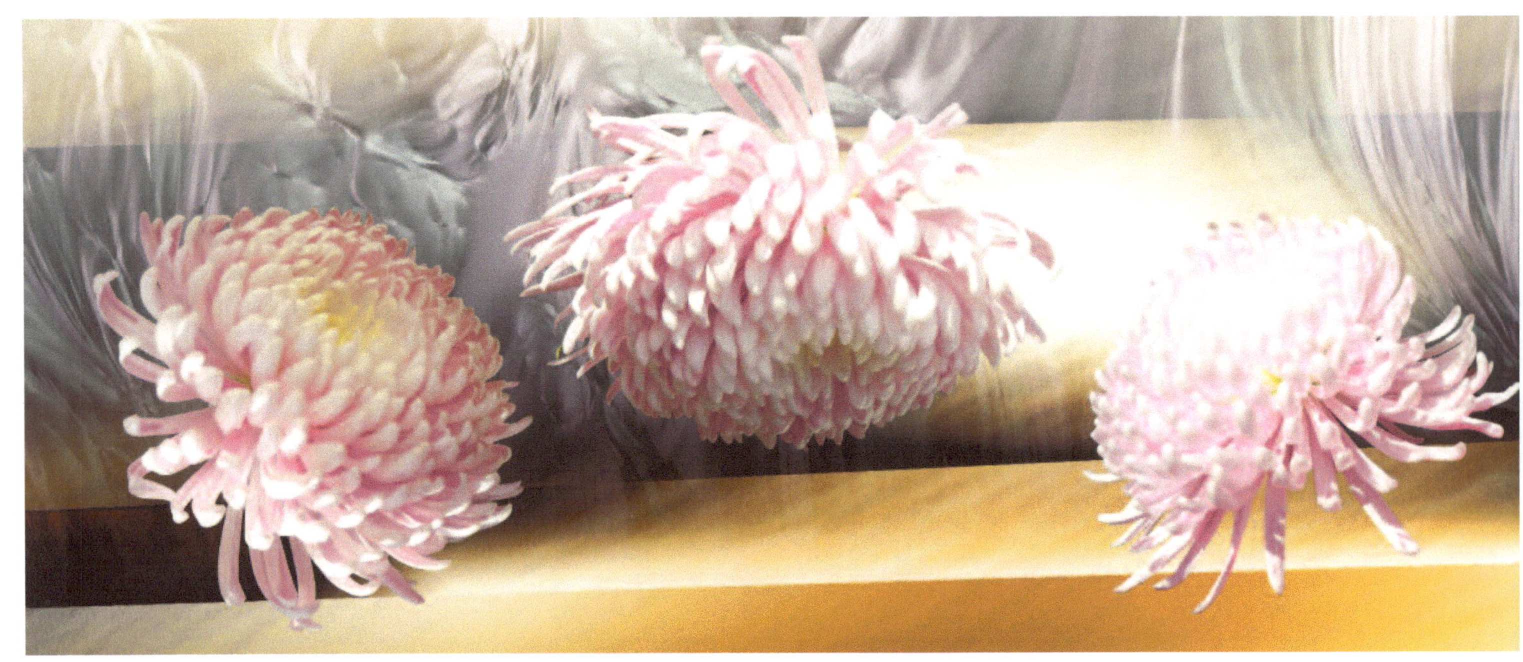

Intercession, digital print on canvas, 18x42 inch

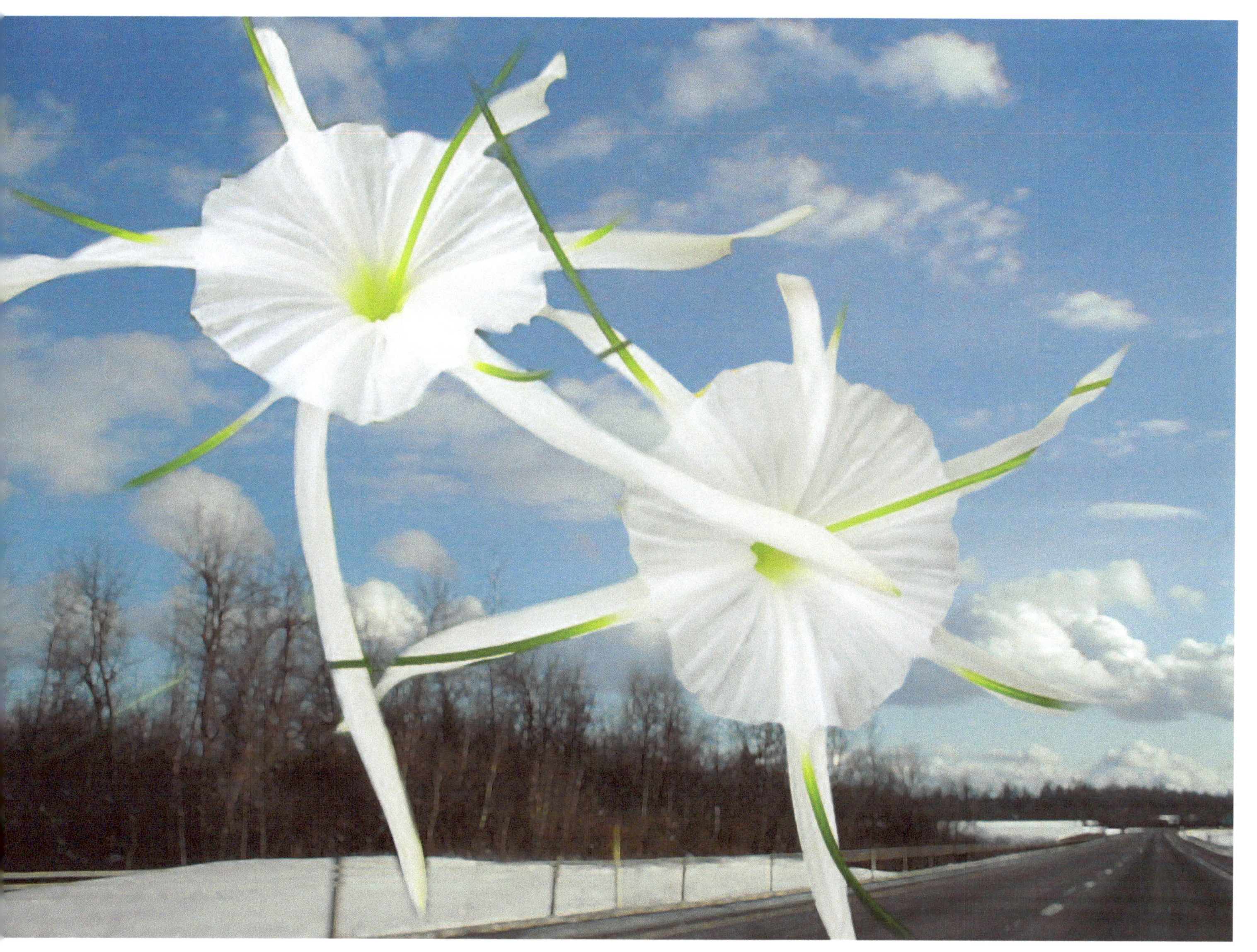

Divine Encounter, digital print on metal, 18x24 inch

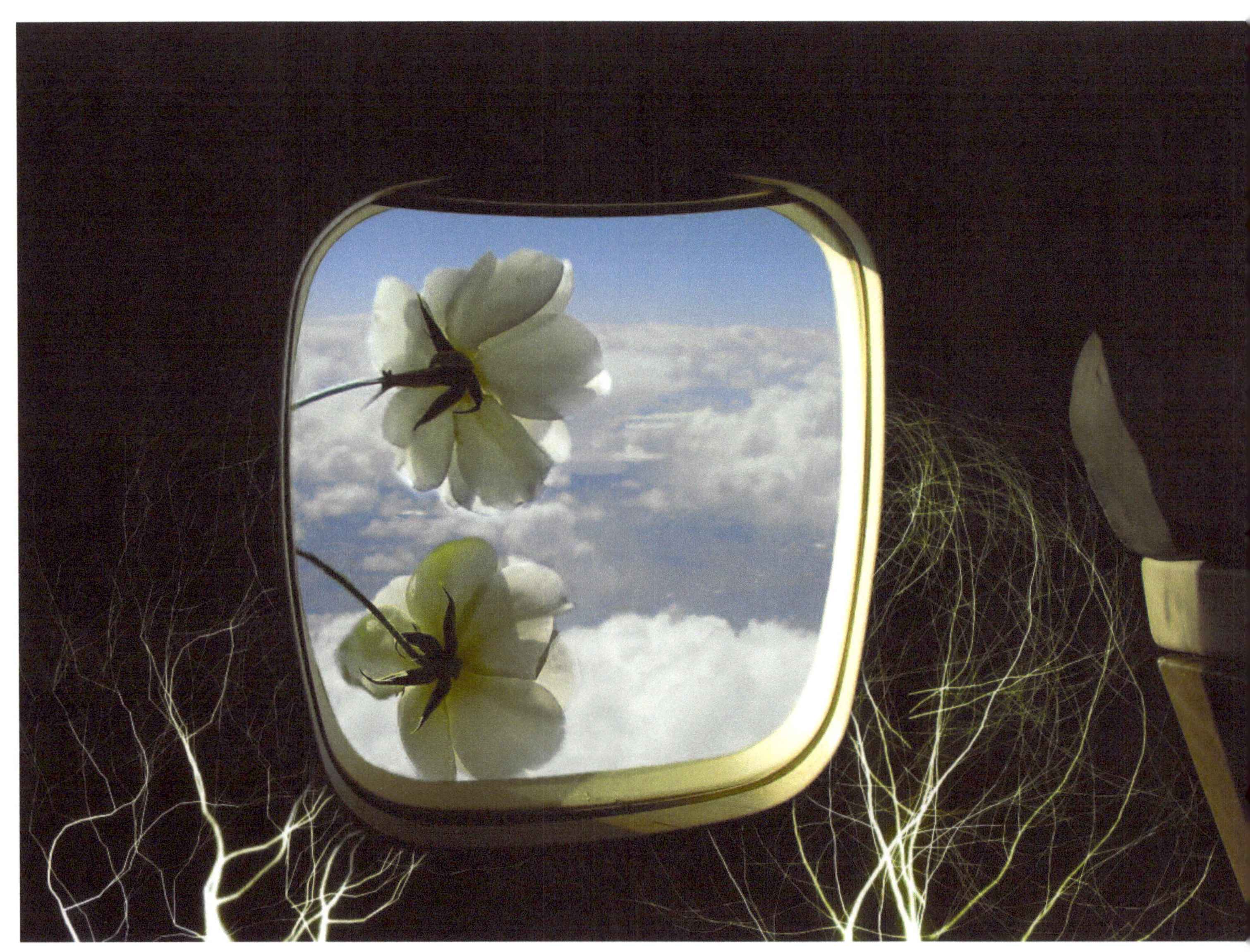

Lifted Soul, digital print on canvas, 18x24 inch

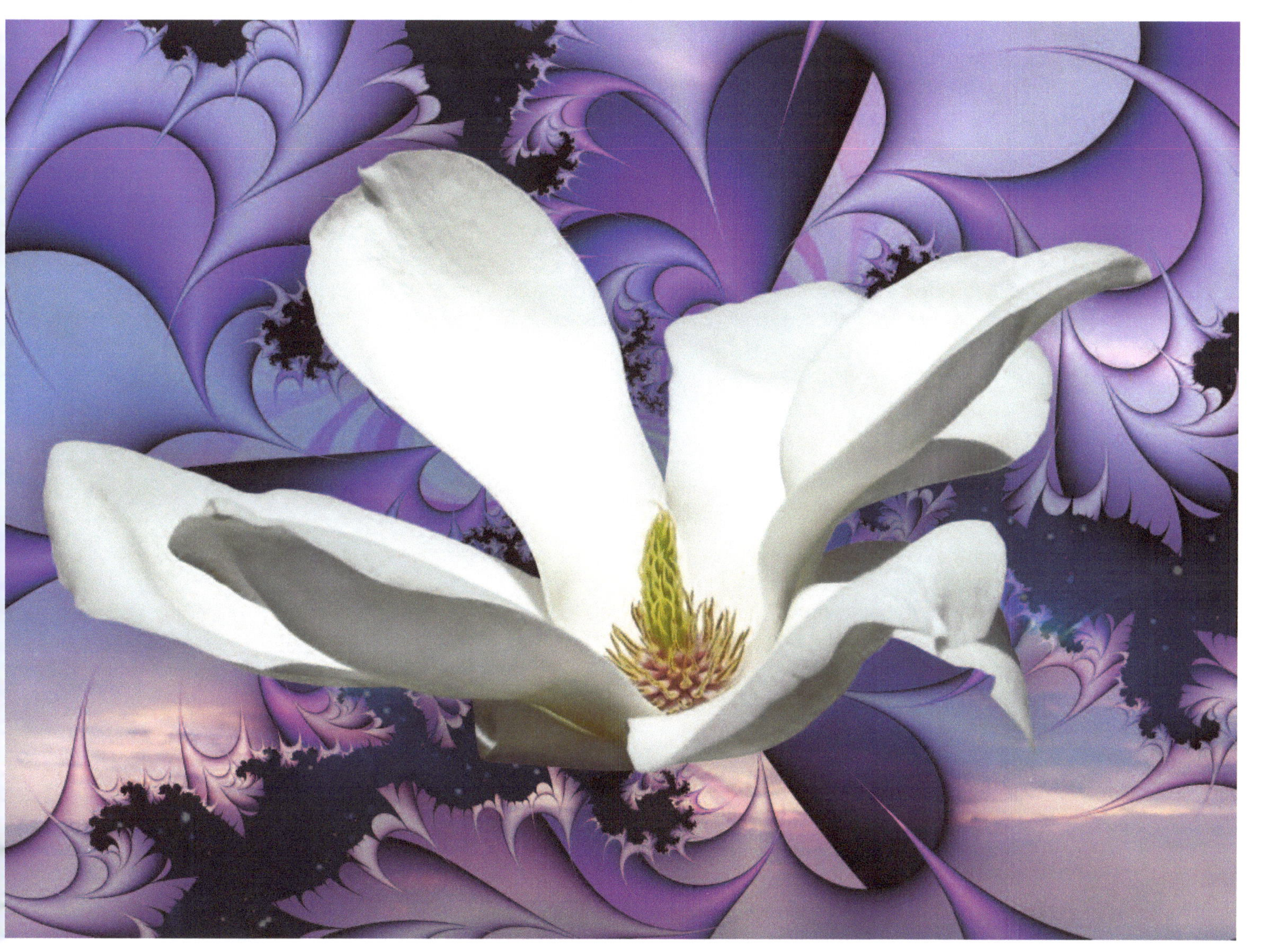

Rise Above, digital print on canvas, 20x27 inch

Statement about Work Process-Mae Jeon

I create images about mind and feelings with digital medium by recapturing my emotional and spiritual experience. In the journey of the digital space I often feel awe at the sight scene as revealing unearthly form and evolved color flow in the space. There I often encountering the abstract scene that evoke my suppressed feeling and spark an inspiration for my art.

Flower has been my primary subject since I began using digital medium for fine art.

Cursive circle form and delicate structure, soft silk skin petals, the flowers remind me a person with feeling. I see the similarity between human emotion and frailty in flower and I found them as a perfect object for representing my unborn image of feelings in spiritual or emotional subject.

I want my chosen flower to play the role of expressing scripted emotion and feeling in my art. The flower in my art isn't simply beautiful flower, rather I want them to play the role of representing an emotion or a feeling in the stage.

Finding a flower for new piece gives me an accidental joy and excitement. I collect the flower images with my digital camera. Then I place the chosen flower into the abstract image for an emotional environment which I captured from my journey in digital space. By combining I rework in the Photoshop or Painter software incorporating or manipulating with plug in filters, and finish image as a whole picture.

My goal in creating art is depicting spiritual states, minds and emotion as visual color and form. I hope I can create the pleasing and beautiful space by combining beauty of object with my idea, and I hope I can make highest quality art as the digital medium in my time allow me in art creation.

Manifesto sul processo creativo di Mae Jeon

Creo immagini di mente e sentimenti con il mezzo digitale riprendendo la mia esperienza emotiva e spirituale. Nel viaggio nello spazio digitale, spesso provo stupore per la scena della vista, rivelando una forma ultraterrena e un flusso di colore evoluto nello spazio. Lì incontro spesso la scena astratta che evoca il mio sentimento represso e accende l'ispirazione per la mia arte.

Il fiore è stato il mio soggetto principale da quando ho iniziato a usare il supporto digitale per le belle arti.

Forma del cerchio ricorsivo e struttura delicata, morbidi petali di seta, i fiori mi ricordano una persona con sentimenti. Vedo la somiglianza tra emozione umana e fragilità in fiore e li ho trovati come un oggetto perfetto per rappresentare la mia immagine non nata di sentimenti in soggetto spirituale o emotivo.

Voglio che il mio fiore scelto reciti il ruolo di esprimere emozioni e sentimenti sceneggiati nella mia arte. Il fiore nella mia arte non è semplicemente un bel fiore, piuttosto voglio che interpretino il ruolo di rappresentare un'emozione o un sentimento sul palcoscenico.

Trovare un fiore per un nuovo pezzo mi dà una gioia ed eccitazione accidentale. Raccolgo le immagini dei fiori con la mia fotocamera digitale. Poi metto il fiore scelto nell'immagine astratta per un ambiente emotivo che ho catturato dal mio viaggio nello spazio digitale. Combinando rielaboro nel software Photoshop o Painter incorporando o manipolando i filtri plug-in e rifinendo l'immagine come immagine intera.

Il mio obiettivo nel creare arte è rappresentato da stati, menti ed emozioni spirituali come colore e forma visiva. Spero di poter creare uno spazio bello e piacevole combinando la bellezza dell'oggetto con la mia idea, e spero di poter fare arte di altissima qualità dato che il mezzo digitale dei miei tempi mi consente di creare arte.

Mae Jeon: 47 Selkirk Street, Staten Island, NY 10309 USA - maejeon@gmail.com www.maejeon.com

EXHIBITION - MOSTRE

SOLO SHOW - MOSTRE PERSONALI

2016 Spectrum Miami, Florida; 2015 Berkeley College Midtown Gallery, NYC, NY; 2014 Artifact Gallery, NYC, NY; 2012 Artists Haven Gallery, Ft. Lauderdale, FL; 2010 ETG Book Café, Staten Island, NY; 2008 Museum of the Americas, Miami, FL; 2007 Art Expo New York, Javits center, NYC; 2006 World Fine Art Gallery, Chelsea, NYC; 2003 Spoke the Hub Re-Creation Center, Brooklyn, NY

SELECTED GROUP SHOW - MOSTRE COLLETTIVE SELEZIONATE

2017 Alliance Fracaise, Small is Beautiful, Dubai, UAE; Noho Gallery, 3rd World Fine Art Agency exhibit, Chelsea, NYC; Impulse Art Inc., Woman in the art, First Prize Award, Houston, TX; 2016 Museo Nazionale, 50 Contemporary Women in the Art, Villa Pisani, Italy; Villa Orsini, The Mural for the Peace, Venice, Italy; Gallera La Pigna Palazzo Maffel Maresotti, Leonardo Da Vinci Award, Rome, Italy; Pleiades Gallery, Spring Fever, Chelsea, NYC; Houdson Guild Gallery, The Somewhere Project, NYC; Hispanic Cultural Institute, Houston, TX; Aurora Studios, Houston, TX; 2015 Paul Kolker Galley, Chelea, NYC; Phoenix Gallery, Chelsea, NYC; The Mural for the Peace, Houston, TX & Oud Metha, Dubai; Berkeley College Brooklyn Gallery, Brooklyn, NY; Sky Light Gallery, Chelsea, NYC; 2014 Carrousal Du Louvre, Art Shopping, Paris France; Art Expo New York, Pier 94, NYC; Latino Art Museum, International Print Festival, Pomona, CA; Museum of the Americas, 100 Certificated Artists, Miami, FL; 2013 Spectrum New York, Javits Center North, NYC; Chianciano Art Museum, Chianciano International Biennale, Tuscany, Italy; New York Art Connection, Long Island, NY; Museum of the Americas, Miami Awards Show, Miami, FL

On back cover: Best Wishes, digital print on metal, 30" circle